diehard

ISBN 0 946230 27 7

The Scottish Pearl in its World Context

Fred Woodward

About the Author

Fred Woodward

Member of European Invertebrates Survey and of Bern Invertebrates Specialist Group, Molluscan Specialist Group of the Species Suurvival Commission for the International Union for the Conservation of Nature, Member & former President of Conchological Society of Great Britain and Ireland, Fellow of Linnaean Society.

His other recent book is *Identifying Shells:* Apple Press 1993, ISBN 1 85076 431 X.

D1407398

The
Scottish Pearl
In Its World Context

Fred Woodward

diehard
Edinburgh
mxmiv

diehard
publishers
3 Spittal Street
Edinburgh
EH3 9DY

ISBN 0 946230 27 7
Copyright Fred Woodward 1994

British Library Cataloguing in Publication Data
A catalog record for this book is
available from the British Library

Our thanks are due to:-
          All the Scottish pearl fishers
who have provided information, including those who
are not mentioned in the text; The Linnaean Society
and their librarian Gina Douglas, for access and help
with Linnaeus' archives; Mr. N. Isaacs and the British
Gemmological Society; Museum and Conchological
colleagues; the Biological Recording in Scotland
Project; Amie Brautigan of the Species Survival
commission for I.U.C.N.; Scottish Natural Heritage;
Mr. Martin Young of Cairncross Ltd, Perth; John
McMillan for the translations from German; and all
others who have been quoted or who have helped.
And to my wife and family for the suffering involved.
F.W.

Foreword

The Freshwater mussel is a biological indicator of the health of our rivers: it is also the highly prized quarry of pearl fishermen, and in Scotland there is a common right to fish for them. There are few such privileges given to the ordinary person, above the rights of the riparian owner, and it is significant, as public access to Scotland's wilderness areas is now a major political issue, that we now know that this right is no longer sustainable, if the Scottish pearl mussel is to survive.

Traditionally the pearl fisher killed every mussel in the search for the elusive and valuable pearl. It is this, in the context of the longevity and slow growth rate of **Margaritifera margaritifera,** *which made it obvious to Scotland's small group of professional fishermen that they needed to devise a method which did not involve killing the mussel. This they succeeded in doing by developing tongs which prise open the shell-halves sufficiently to allow inspection and removal of a pearl from the mussel's mantle without harming it. Unfortunately, it was impossible to communicate this method to the much larger number of amateur pearl fishermen, and it therefore became necessary to introduce legislation in 1989 to protect the animal by making it illegal to kill them.*

Fred Woodward is the champion of **Margaritifera margaritifera.** *His interest in its natural history, its exploitation by man since pre-Roman times, its global context, and the politics needed to ensure its survival, is the subject of this book. His main concern is for its* *wellbeing and yet he manages to introduce an elegiac sympathy for the Scottish group of professional pearl fishers, Bill Abernethy, Peter Goodwin and the McCormack family.*

The 1992 Rio conference on the global environment highlighted the issue of biodiversity, and it is therefore important that each threatened species has its champions. Fred Woodward's commitment is much more important than championing the cause of a single species however, because his holistic approach has more in common with the Scottish biologist and philosopher, Patrick Geddes, in the way he invites us to think globally and act locally. **Margaritifera margaritifera** *is more than yet another threatened species or a biological indicator; ultimately it is a measure of our commitment to sustaining our environment.*

Tony Andrews
April 1994

Tony Andrews, a riparian owner, is Director of the British Council, Scotland, in which capacity he is about to set up a project which will include river management in the Kola Peninsula, Russia.

CONTENTS

INTRODUCTION

Man has collected molluscs and their shells since prehistoric times over 30,000 years ago, for food, as tools, for medicine or personal adornment, or simply for their beauty or rarity.

Shell remains, present in Bronze Age and mediaeval settlements, such as limpets, oysters and land-snails, testify to their use as a food source, whilst others, such as cowries, conches and fragments of mother-of-pearl, indicate an intrinsic value which continues with our own high esteem of cameos and pearls.

W. Harrison Hutton in a paper given to the Leeds Conchological Club in November 1917 writes:

One of the earliest records of pearls as ornaments is of a number of mother-of-pearl inlaid ornaments found amongst the ruins of Bismaya (Babylon?) which dated from 4,500 B.C. Specimens of worked mother-of-pearl have frequently been found at Thebes, Egypt, some dating back to 3,200 B.C.; and a very beautiful necklace of pearls and gold, dated 300 B.C. is in the Museum of Art, New York. In 88 B.C. pearls were very popular in Rome, so popular that acts of the Senate had to be passed restricting and controlling the wearing of them. Their use is mentioned in the Vedas, one of the very ancient gospels of India, where they were used as armlets around 500 B.C. and were believed to have great and potent power to protect the wearer, giving strength, long life and lustiness. They were listed as a product of China with a number of other products in 550 B.C., and in Shu-King, one of the ancient books of China, are records of pearls in 625 B.C.

Also in some of the old books of Persia is mention of pearls dating back to 700 B.C. About A.D. 768-814, pearls were largely used in decorating the bindings of missals, manuscripts, etc. The Sahburnham MS of the four gospels, in the possession of the Piedmont Morgan family, is a very wonderful and beautiful example : it contains 98 fine freshwater pearls on the bindings. In ecclesiastical decoration, pearls have always been largely used, and are still much used, mostly freshwater pearls. Pliny states that the Romans used the word 'Unio' to distinguish a large perfect one from a smaller and less attractive one; these were called *Margarita*.

In ancient times freshwater mussel shells were also considered of value due to their pearly interior and often occur in archaeological sites in Greece dating from about 2,000 B.C. Such shells were often pierced for use as pendants or, in some cases, the two valves were attached together to form a pearly container. This practice continued until Roman times as evidenced by the discovery of two valves belonging to the related genus **Unio** in the debris of an officer's rooms, during the excavations of the Arbeia Roman Fort at South Shields, Tyne and Wear, in the mid 1970's.

Two species of **Unio** occur in Britain, the Painter's Mussel, **Unio pictorum**, so named from its use to contain artists' colours in the eighteenth century, and the Tumid Mussel, **Unio tumidus**, both of which are absent from Scotland and Ireland. In the case of the Arbeia Roman Fort **Unio**, however, the species was **Unio crassus** which is now restricted to the European continent although its remains are present as fossils in the English Pleistocene. It would seem probable that the Roman owner had brought these shells with him from the continent to South Shields at the end of the first century A.D.

What are Pearls?

A Pearl may be defined as a hard, smooth, lustrous, typically rounded structure occurring on the inner shell surface or embedded in the tissues of molluscs. The pearl itself consists of a series of concentric layers of calcium carbonate which have been secreted by the animal, usually around an intrusive particle such as a sandgrain or parasite. Pearls generally occur in bivalves but may also be found in gastropods and cephalopods. From a biological aspect there are two types of pearly bodies. The first of these, 'blister pearls', are excrescences on the interior of the shell formed to close holes made by shell-boring animals, or to coat over natural intrusive objects such as grains of sand, small crabs, etc.. These form a group together with Buddha 'pearls', Linnaeus 'pearls', and the 'half pearls' originally produced by Mr. Mikimoto, and metal images or beads. Over such a blister the epidermis forms a little pocket, directly continuous with the shell secreting epithelium.

True *pearls* are formed in a closed sac of shell-secreting epidermis, embedded in the tissues of the oyster, the nacre-secreting surface of which is not continuous with that of the epidermis that lays down the shell itself. A blister is a more or less hemispherical body passing over on all sides into the shell substance; a pearl is a concentrically deposited body , the substance of which is nowhere continuous with that of the shell.

A pearl may, in the course of time, be ejected into the space between mantle and shell, and become more or less buried in the shell, forming the core of a blister; but in that case can be dissected out from the shell layers deposited over it.

B. B. Woodward in *The Life of the Mollusca* (1913), writes:

Their other modern uses for ornamental purposes, as well known, are extensive and varied - from ash trays to Mother-of-Pearl inlaying work, while pearls form an additional item apart, and have been highly esteemed from very early times. These are not only from the Pearl Oyster of Ceylon and the East, but are met with in the freshwater Pearl Mussel (**Margaritana margaritifer**), and their fishing once formed a valuable industry; while the occurrence of pearls in the Zebra Mussel (**Dreissenia**) in Staffordshire has been recorded. Indeed, the Romans seem to have held the British freshwater Pearls in high estimation; while, according to Pliny, Caesar dedicated to Venus Genetrix, and hung in her temple at Rome, a breastplate covered with British pearls, though these were possibly from the marine Mussel, which, as well as the Oyster, sometimes yields pearls. A large dull kind of pearl is also got from **Tridacna** (the Giant Clam), and pink pearls from the West Indian Fountain shell (**Strombus gigas**), as well as from certain **Turbinella**. Fossil pearls of large size have, moreover, been found in our English chalk, being the product of the big Bivalve (**Inoceramus**). Dr. Willey was fortunate enough to obtain a large pearl from a **Nautilus** shell in New Britain, this being apparently the only one known.

Origin of Pearls

The origin of pearls has been the subject of debate throughout the centuries. One of the old beliefs was that a pearl was a solidified dewdrop. Thus Camden, *Britannia* (1551-1623) says:

The rivers in Conway, Wales, breed a kind of shell which being [im]pregnated with dew, produces pearls.

J. S. Schroeter, treating this subject in 1779 writes:

I would be long-winded if I were to repeat all the opinions which I have heard on the origin of pearls, some of which are tasteless and laughable. I will quote the two newest opinions but I make the assertion that the theory of Herr Chemnitz holds the most worth. According to his theory, the pearls are protection against hostile attack, and healing-plaster for wounds. The objection to this, that one also finds pearls in the animal itself, appears to me not to be as important as is believed. If the mussel-animal has the intelligence to know that it is injured, and then works to overcome it, then it seems to me not unreasonable to believe that the animal could have one more pearl on hand to lay down in the area of the wound. What, then, is the pearl-material? All believe that it is at least the foundation-material of true pearls, which is used by the animal to protect itself when it has no true pearls on hand. I have seen a common oyster, in which half of the inside of one shell was covered with a club-shaped swelling, which is hollow in the middle. The animal could check promptly any hostile creature.

According to Chemnitz's theory, the pearls are protective material against fatal wounds, and healing plaster of previous wounds...

Here I must take leave of Herr Pastor Chemnitz's theory on the origin of pearls. If we accept that pearls are preservation material and healing plaster, then it is to be expected that undamaged and unpunctured shells are in all probability unfruitful of pearls. There are, on the contrary, shells which have suffered great injury, and the probability of them containing a pearl is just the same. How desirable it would be, if one could, by this characteristic, confirm or refute the existence of a pearl.

The other theory on the origin of pearls which I will quote was postulated by Herr Gissler in the Journal of the Swedish Academy in 1762. I repeat a few of his thoughts on the matter, so that anyone who can clarify them may do so.

"The pearl is originally a round, very small, clear piece of mother-of-pearl which is secreted by the animal and built up in the same manner as the shell. It is held onto the shell by a slice of the skin."
So much appears to be right:-

"The internal film of the shell, including the pearls, consists of one composite layer, and the pearl itself consists of built-up layers. The pearl originates, though, from the finest elements, which are rarer than those of the shell. This matches Herr Chemnitz's theory, as he states that the animal gives its best material to the pearl, so that it may be very strong, in order to be a plaster in the wound, and prevent any attack from foreign bodies."

Schroeter continues:

The position of the pearls is also variable. They are either fixed in the shell, or they lie free in the animal, without any fastening. In this latter case, according to Herr Hofmedicus Taube, they lie between the skin of the so-called 'beard' of the mussel or, just as often, are found lying between the inner skins of the animal. Could it be, that the pearl grows in the shell, sitting quite firmly, so that the hidden underside is not ripe? Pearls, however, are found in this condition, lying free in the shell. Whether it is right that the pearl leaves its site in the mussel shell when it is ripe, I can neither confirm nor refute. I lack personal experience and new evidence, and the evidence of the older writers is, in this case, not firm.

Mostly, our river-mussels contain only one, or at best, two, pearls, although some examples do contain more. We can certainly say of our freshwater mussels, that they do not approach the mussels described by Ameritus Vespucius and Caspar Morales, the former having found mussels with 130 pearls, and the latter mussels with 120.

W. Dall writes in the *American Naturalist* for June 1883:

Pearls are concretions in the tissues, of the same material as that which composes the shell-layers, and are usually due to the presence, in the secreting tissue, of some irritating particle or parasite, such as in the tissues of an animal a **Trichina** becomes covered with a limy cyst. In the Mollusk, however, the layers are constantly added to until the pearl reaches a considerable size. When it becomes so large that the valves of the shell cannot close, the Mollusk soon dies and the pearl may be washed away and lost. If the pearl escapes from the tissues during the life of the animal it may become cemented to the inside of the valves; or pseudo-pearls may be formed by the mantle over projections from the inside of the valves. Concretions similar to pearls, but lustreless, are formed in many molluscs, as in the Oyster. Upon the part of the mantle which makes the deposit the character of the pearl depends. Some of the concretions partake of the nature of the epidermis, are brown or yellow, without lustre. Most freshwater pearls when sawn in two, show an aggregation of prismatic shell substance radiating from a central point, which alternates with concentric epidermal layers and is externally covered with a layer of true pearl. If the last is thick, clear and iridescent the pearl is valuable, if not, worthless. The common notion of a pearl being pearly throughout, is mostly incorrect. Disease may set up an irritation which will cause shelly concretions to form in the tissues of the Mollusk. These are usually small and irregularly shaped and in the pearl mussel are most frequent in the substance of the large muscles which close the valves. Such are called sand-pearls and are mostly used in embroidery and cheap jewellery. In these cases the pearl lies in the substance of the mantle or tissues, but it may, with increasing size, work out into the cavity of the shell outside the mantle. It is then apt to become attached to the inside of the shell. These are less valuable because less regular in shape and iridescence than free pearls. In any case the matter of which the pearl is composed is secreted at the expense of the shell, so that it is not strange that a shell containing two good-sized pearls is always recognizable and it is seldom that a shell of perfectly regular shape contains a pearl. The fishers say that three characters externally show the presence of pearls. *1st* grooves or ridges from the beaks to the margin. *2nd* a kidney-shaped outline. *3rd* the asymmetry of the valves with regard to the median vertical plane of the animal.

B. B. Woodward suggests one possible reason for pearl production as a result of the mussel's infection by a parasite. He writes (again in *The Life of the Mollusca*):

The nucleus frequently consists of a fragment of a brownish-yellow organic substance which behaves in the same way as epidermis when treated with certain chemical reagents. Sand is generally said to be the nucleus; but this is simply a conjecture which has gradually become regarded as a fact; it is quite the exception for sand to be the nucleus; as a general rule it is some organic substance. In some districts one kind of nucleus seems to be more common than another; at least this is how the different results obtained by observers in different localities may be explained. Filippi (*Sull' origine delle Perle*, translated in Muller's Archive 1856), found **Distoma** to be the nucleus in many cases; Kirchenmeister found that pearls were most abundant in the Molluscs living in the still parts of the River Elster, where the water-mites (**Limnochares anodontae**) existed most numerously. The most generally prevalent nucleus appears to be the bodies of eggs of minute internal parasites such as **Filaria, Distoma, Bucephalus**, etc. Completely spherical pearls can only be found loose in the muscles or other soft parts of the animal. The Chinese obtain them artificially by introducing into the living mussel foreign substances such as pieces of mother-of-pearl fixed to wires, which thus become coated with a more brilliant material. Pearls are similar in structure to the shell, and like it consist of three layers; but what is the innermost layer in the shell is placed on the outside in the pearl. The iridescence is due to light falling upon the outcropping edges of partially transparent corrugated plates. The thinner and more transparent the plates, the more beautiful is the iridescent lustre; and this is said to be the reason why sea-pearls excel those obtained from freshwater molluscs. Besides the furrows formed by the corrugated surface there are a number of fine dark lines (1/7700 inch apart) which may add to the lustrous effect. In some pearls these lines run from pole to pole like the longitudes on the globe; in others they run in various directions, so that they cross each other.

He continues:

Among molluscan parasites the most abundant belong to the stages of Platyhelminthian Worms, which complete the cycle of their existence in some other animal, such as Birds, Fish, Frogs, etc. The history of these is completely known in but few cases. ....Still more interesting is the fact that the pearl of commerce has been said to owe its existence to the action of a Cestode larva (**Tetrarhychyus**), which completes its life-cycle in the bodies of two successive kinds of Fish that prey, the one on the Pearl Oysters, the other on its fellow, as well as on the Oysters. The supposition is that, if the embryo worm, on forcing its way into the tissues of the mollusc, carries with it some of the epithelial cells of the latter, an abnormal growth of pearl-secreting cells within the tissues of the animal results, and a pearl is formed, having the parasite for its central point.

Colour

Schroeter writes:

> The colour of the pearls is quite variable. The most beautiful pearls must have a beautiful lustre, i.e. they must be beautifully white and shining, and half transparent. This feature is called by Plinius *Exaluminatos Uniones*.
>
> In reality, this is rare. Most are merely white without shine, others have a shine, but their colour is not white enough. Sometimes they are brown, or not entirely of one colour. Only the first sort have any worth, the others are only good for the 'Kabinett', or for other sorts of art work. Thus we have in our Ducal Kabinett here in Weimar, a brown pearl of considerable size, which has been carved into the shape of a little castle.

The colours exhibited by a pearl are produced as a result of diffraction of light by the minute nacreous crystals which make up the pearl, with the result that colours vary considerably, depending upon crystal size, chemical composition, position of origin within the mussel tissues, locality of the mussel concerned, etc. However freshwater pearls possess an unexplainable quality which distinguishes them from marine pearls to a trained eye. Indeed some claim that it is even possible to determine the river from which a particular pearl originates by its shape and colour. The late Alastair Cairncross, the Perth jeweller and goldsmith and leading authority on Scottish freshwater pearls, has outlined the characteristic of a Scottish pearl as follows:

> The beauty of the pearl lies in its fineness of orient, its quality of lustre and body colour. This depends on many factors - where the mussel has been living, chemicals in the water, and feeding matter.

Colours vary considerably from white through greys to gold and lilac. When compared with oriental pearls, the Scots pearl is like a plum still on the tree with the bloom on it, while the former are plums picked from the trees, polished and put in a shop window.

There is a lovely untouched quality about them which is highly distinctive, so that they are obviously real and cannot be mistaken for anything other than what they are.

In contrast to natural freshwater and marine pearls, cultured pearls tend to be uniform in colour and in the majority of cases are subsequently stained to produce a uniform coloration for grading. Evidence of this staining may be discerned by examination of the drill holes. In addition such artificially stained pearls tend to discolour, a process which can occur after as little as five years. Such pearls obviously will tend to lose their value.

CULTURED PEARLS

Chinese River Pearls

Pearls have been highly valued in China from a very early period. Many pearls mentioned by Chinese historians as remarkable for their size and brilliance were of marine origin but some were undoubtedly freshwater. Chan, the inventor of the compass, writing in the 8th century, refers to pearls being produced in the inland province of Shensi. About 1850, the Scot, Dr. Macgowan, records that Chinese freshwater pearl production is confined to the villages of Chung-kwan and Siau-chang-ngan in the silk-producing region near Tehtsing, in the northern part of Chihkiang.

In May or June, large quantities of mussels (**Mytilus cygnus** [= **Dipsas plicatus** (Leach)]), are brought from Tahu, a lake in Kiangsu, about thirty miles distant, and placed in bamboo cages for a few days to recover from their journey. The largest are then selected to receive the pearl nuclei which vary in form and materials, the commonest being made of mud from the bottom of the pond or river. This is dried, powdered with the juice of camphor-tree seeds, and formed into pills which when dry, are introduced into the unfortunate mussel. The best nuclei are brought from Canton and appear to be made from the shell of the marine Pearl-oyster. Irregular shell fragments are ground with sand in a iron mortar, until they become smooth and globular. Other nuclei consist of small images usually of Buddha or a fish. These are of thinly cast lead made by pouring onto an impressed board. Pearls having these forms caused considerable interest when first encountered by Europeans in the 1800's.

The introduction of pearl nuclei is a considerably delicate operation. The shell is opened with a spatula of Mother-of-Pearl, and the free portion of the mollusc carefully separated from one surface of the shell with an iron probe; the nuclei are then successively introduced on the end of a bifurcated bamboo stick, and placed in two parallel rows on the animal's mantle surface. A sufficient number having been placed on one side, the operation is repeated on the other. The nuclei cause the animal to spasmodically press against both sides of its shell, keeping the nuclei in place. The nucleated mussels are placed singly in streams or pools, five or six inches apart, at depths of from one to five feet, in lots of from five to fifty thousand.

The shells are collected in November, the animal removed, and the Pearls detached by a sharp knife. If the pearl nucleus is of nacre it is left in but earthen and metallic nuclei are cut away, melted yellow resin poured into the cavity, and the hole artfully sealed by a piece of Mother-of-Pearl. These 'blister-pearls' possess the lustre and beauty of the solid gem, being produced so cheaply as to be procurable by anyone caring to own them. They are generally purchased by jewellers and others, who set them in tiaras, circlets and various ornaments of female attire. Those formed on the image of Buddha are finished in the same manner, and used as ornaments and amulets on the caps of small children. A few shells are retained with their adhering Pearls, for sale to the curious or superstitious, specimens of which have by this time found their way into the principal public and private cabinets of Europe and America. A tinge of yellow is found over the whole inner surface of some shells, shewing that the more recent secretion of nacre by the animal was unnatural; the flesh of all, however, is eaten.

Some five thousand families were engaged in this industry but chiefly derived their income from cultivating mulberry, rearing silkworms, or other agricultural operations. Those not expert in the management of the shells lose ten to fifteen per cent by death; others lose none in a whole season.

The method used is attributed by the villagers to a native of the place, ancestor of many of them, named Yu Shun-yang, to whom a temple has been erected, in which divine honours are paid to him. He lived at the end of the fourteenth century.

Schroeter also recorded this industry in 1779 thus:

I only wish further to quote Herr Grill's report, on how the Chinese cultivate regal pearls, and enlarge existing examples. According to Herr Grill , 'in the early summer, the mussels come to the surface of the water, and open and lie in the sun. The Chinese take a string, onto which are tied five or six small pearls, a little apart from each other. Into each open mussel, they place such a string. The mussels, loaded with this strange burden, close, and sink into the water. Some time later the mussels are brought to the surface, and on their being opened, each of the small pearls is found to have been covered with new pearl-skin, and have all the appearance of real pearls.....'

Professor Murray of Uppsala told me of this some years ago, with a few differences. He explains that the mussels of the Chinese rivers occasionally come to the surface. The Chinese take advantage of this, by throwing into each open mussel a little round ball which has been turned from mother-of-pearl. They do this with wondrous and extraordinary skill. As soon as the mussel has the little ball inside, it sinks to the bottom. The following year, there is found a beautiful pearl for each little ball. Perhaps the mussel has assumed it has been wounded, and has striven to protect itself?

Chinese freshwater pearl production recommenced in the late 1960's with such success that China is now the chief world producer with a yield averaging between fifty to eighty tons per year compared with a mere five tons for Japanese producers.

In Europe, the Swedish naturalist Linnaeus, famous for his introduction of a binomial system for animal and plant classification used to the present day, improved upon the Chinese method for producing 'blister-pearls' as shown by his report to the Swedish Secret Committee in 1761. Using the Painters Mussel, **Unio pictorum**, he introduced spherical nuclei composed of plaster, stone or unslaked lime into the space between the shell valve and the mantle lobe by boring a hole through the shell. In addition this nucleus was diagonally perforated and a silver wire threaded through in order to elevate the nucleus above the valve surface. The insertion hole was then closed on the outside by a piece of shell and the animal then placed back in the river bed and left for about six years. After this period it was removed and the resultant pearl, which was virtually in the round, removed. Examples of Linnaeus' pearls still exist in the collections of the Linnaean Society of London and prove to be of a high quality and far in advance of anything produced until the twentieth century.

Linnaeus offered his method to Sweden but his offer was turned down, being taken up on his country's behalf by Peter Bagge, a Swedish merchant, who failed to put the process into operation during his lifetime. In 1820 his grandson, J. P. Bagge, was granted permission to use the process, but it is not known whether he actually did so.

Significantly, other European scientists also attempted to simulate Linnaeus, including the eminent Scottish physician, Dr. John Hunter, whose collections form the basis of the Museum of the Royal College of Surgeons (those of his brother William forming the Hunterian Museum Collections at Glasgow University).

John wrote to Sir Joseph Banks from Leicester Square on the 10th April 1787, stating that he had been draining the pond (at Earl's Court) and fishing for pearls, of which he sends specimens; the [molluscs] on which he experimented are dead, but he has others alive which he will submit for experiments and hopes to get larger pearls. In the same letter he continues to say that he has lately got a 'Tall Man' which he hopes to show to Banks next summer. This is presumed to refer to the skeleton of Charles Byrne, the Irish Giant, which Hunter acquired in 1783 and is still in the collections at the Royal College of Surgeons. Whether any of John Hunter's cultivated pearls still exist is uncertain.

The techniques employed for the production of cultivated pearls remained virtually unaltered until the beginning of the twentieth century. The pearls produced were simply blister pearls. This changed dramatically in the 1920's with the introduction of Mikimoto's implantation method for the cultivation of marine pearls.

MIKIMOTO CULTURED MARINE PEARLS

On May 4, 1921, a London evening paper announced that quantities of artificially produced Japanese pearls, of perfectly spherical shape, but containing in their centres beads of mother-of-pearl, had found their way into the London market and had deceived experienced pearl merchants in Hatton Garden, who had bought and resold them as naturally produced gems.

For some years Mr. K. Mikimoto, the pioneer in the application of scientific knowledge to the pearl oyster on a commercial scale, had been producing in Japan, and selling under the name of 'Mikimoto pearls' pearls of this description. There was no secret about this. Mr. Mikimoto not only sold them as artificially produced pearls, but also published in one of his catalogues a short description and diagram explaining his process.

Ever since 1898 Mr. Mikimoto (who began his work in collaboration with the late Prof. Mitsukuri in 1890) had been marketing half-pearls or 'blisters', pearly excrescences formed by inserting a mother-of-Pearl bead between the body of the oyster and the shell, and allowing the oyster to coat it over with nacre. This was, of course, merely a development of the very old operation by which the Chinese produce in fresh-water mussels the well-known mother-of-pearl images of Buddha, and of Linnaeus' classical experiments in the eighteenth century. These products were known as 'culture pearls' and have long been familiar in this country, set in brooches, tie-pins, rings etc. Their value, compared with real pearls of corresponding size was, of course, quite small.

For many years Mr. Mikimoto experimented with a view to the production of a complete pearl, not attached to the shell, by a modification of this process, and obtained his first successful results about 1912.

The process involves delicate and skillful manipulation and is carried out by carefully selected and trained workers. The shell is removed from one pearl oyster, and a bead of nacre or other suitable nucleus is laid on the outer shell-secreting epidermis of the mantle. This epidermis, which is composed of a single layer of cells of microscopic size, is then dissected off the oyster, and made to envelop the nucleus as a sac, the neck of which is ligatured. This sac is then transplanted into a second oyster and embedded in its sub-epidermal tissues. The ligature is removed, certain astringents or other reagents are applied to the wound, and the second oyster, with its grafted pearl-sac containing the mother-of-pearl bead, is returned to the sea, where it has to remain for several years before a coating of pearl of sufficient thickness is secreted around the introduced bead.

When a slice is cut across a natural pearl and a Mikimoto pearl the distinction is obvious. A natural pearl consists throughout of concentrically deposited layers, which differ in degree of transparency or opacity in different specimens. The Mikimoto pearl, in its outer layers, has the same structure as the natural pearl, but has an artificially manufactured bead of mother-of-pearl, composed of flat parallel laminae of nacre, in its centre.

The considerable concern expressed by dealers in the 1920's regarding the differentiation between genuine natural pearls and Mikimoto cultured pearls led to the establishment of the Gemmological Testing Centre, which continues to this day. This Centre not only determines the validity of pearls, but also natural gemstones such as diamonds, rubies, garnets, etc., many of which are now capable of being manufactured artificially.

Since Mikimoto's innovation to pearl culture of marine pearls in the round, pearl farms have arisen throughout the world and are found in Polynesia,

Australia, Japan, Ceylon, India, etc., but the product can still be distinguished from the continuingly more valuable natural pearls, due to the nucleus, which may be readily detected with the use of X-rays.

In the late 1960's the Chinese commenced the cultivation of freshwater pearls, using a modification of Mikimoto's method, by implanting mantle tissue from a living mussel into the tissues of another, to induce the development of non-nucleated pearls. These tend to be elongated and misshapen, with the appearance of rice-grains. The production of these is mainly in the area around Shanghai, local freshwater mussels obtained from the nearby rivers being implanted and then impounded in man made ponds, where they remain for two or three years. They are then harvested and the animals placed in tubs and left to decompose. The resulting residue is later washed to obtain the pearls. These are then drilled locally to make necklaces, etc. On average, about eighty tons of these poor quality pearls are exported annually.

The Chinese have also recently resurrected cultivating freshwater blister pearls for use in manufacturing cheap jewellery, by the introduction of small plastic hemispheres to the inner shell surface. The resultant dome of nacre, which takes two or three years to reach a sufficient thickness, is then cut away and filled with resin. This is then backed with a thin slice of nacre and used for ear-rings, pendants, etc.

Finally, India and Thailand have also been producing cultivated freshwater pearls since the 1980's using native species of freshwater mussels. Here again the resultant pearls tend to be of inferior quality and little attention has been given to the maintenance of freshwater mussels in the wild.

IMITATION PEARLS

Imitation pearls have no connection with marine or freshwater pearl mussels being only related to the real article by appearance. The synthetic or imitation pearl industry dates from 1656 when Jacquin, the famous Frenchman, found that water in which a certain fish (**Albinus lucidus**, a species of freshwater bleak) had been washed became clouded with iridescent and glittering spangles, which by long standing and continued washing he was able to obtain in the form of a paste. Noting the pearl-like lustre of this paste, especially when dry, he conceived the idea of coating small hard beads with a mixture of this paste, and so prepared the first imitation pearl. The imitations were apparently successful, and caught on well with the public of the day, since it is recorded that they were the fashionable craze of the time, no lady's jewel box being complete without a string of the new beads. Contemporary literature contains an interesting story of a penniless marquis who tricked a young girl into belief in his pecuniary stability by means of a string of Jacquin's imitation pearls.

A large French industry gradually arose and was referred to by Reaumur in 1716 who noted that the liquid used was a suspension and not a true solution. The pearl essence had to be prepared fresh every few days by fractional washing of fish scales. It was recorded that in thundery weather the essence might purify in a few hours. The method of preservation with concentrated ammonia was apparently not known.

Before the 1939-45 World War the methods of preparation of pearl essence differed little from those used two and a half centuries earlier. On the continent the source of it was various species of bleak, but in Britain it was obtained from the herring

(**Clupea harengus**), the English centre of manufacture being Yarmouth. Fish from the nets were gently washed with water to remove salts and various impurities, the belly scales scraped with the back of a knife and then thrown into a tank of running water, and the pearl essence washed out of the loosened scales obtained by sedimentation. The tiny iridescent platelets readily absorb colouring matter from solution so that the highest cleanliness is necessary in all stages of the operation. The essence may be preserved in aqueous suspension by adding a large excess of ammonia in order to arrest putrefaction. Another method is to suspend the dried plates in a pure organic solvent such as acetone or amyl acetate. This facilitates its conversion into pearl varnishes or artificial mother-of-pearl. However the slightest traces of water will, if present, cause the platelets to clot together in a mass which cannot be dispersed.

Guanine, the purine of pearl essence, is almost universally found in the scales of small fish, and functions as camouflage, a silvery light being reflected from the guanine crystals, which occur chiefly on the underside of the fish, making it almost invisible when viewed from below.

Glass beads to be treated with pearl essence were made in a variety of ways. In cheaper brands a row of bulbs were blown into a mould using colourless soft lead glass, individual beads being severed at the constrictions. This type possessed a ridge on either side and were only used for inferior work.

For external coating, 'solid' beads were made from short lengths of thick-walled capillary tubing heated in a rotating cylindrical vessel filled with talc powder to prevent the softened beads from adhering to one another, the rotation converting them from a cylindrical to a spherical shape. For the best work, thin lamp-blown glass shells were made by a special process, the holes for threading being blown by using a perforated screen. These hollow beads were coated inside by a thin layer of pearl essence in amyl acetate varnish and then filled with coloured wax, but they were easily broken. The 'solid' externally coated beads were not only more realistic but less easily broken, but they had the disadvantage that the coating was liable to wear off.

Imitation pearls can easily be identified by density, true pearls being fairly constant at 2.6, whilst hollow imitations are usually much lighter. Also the holes of a true pearl are drilled, those of an imitation are rounded. True Pearls are faintly iridescent with a matt surface which will not give sharp images of distant objects by reflection, while internally coated pearls exhibit sharp reflected images. True Pearls are unaltered by immersion in amyl acetate, but disintegrate in dilute hydrochloric acid, the reverse being the case with externally-coated imitations.

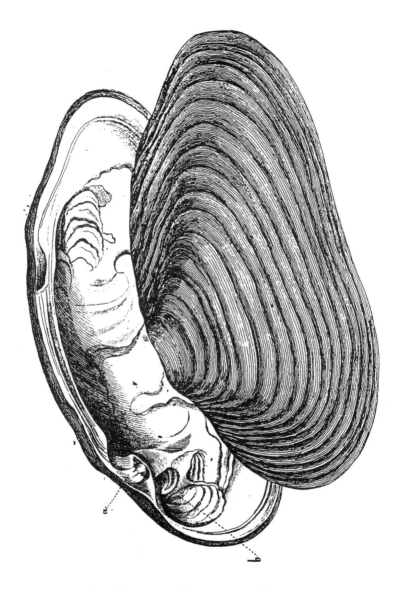

Schroeter's **Mya margaritifera**
or **Margaritifera margaritifera** (Linnaeus)
as it is now known.

THE FRESHWATER PEARL MUSSEL

Scottish freshwater pearls are obtained from the drab looking freshwater pearl mussel, **Margaritifera margaritifera** (Linnaeus), whose shells are often to be seen cast up amongst the debris deposited onto our river banks after periods of severe flood. The accompanying illustration is by Johann Samuel Schroeter, (1735-1808), a Thuringian clergyman who lived his entire life in the vicinity of Weimar and Buttstadt, Germany. Amongst his many publications on molluscs was a large monograph on the freshwater molluscs of Thuringia, published in 1779, from which are taken this illustration and detailed description, as well as numerous observations referred to in this book.

[No. 6] The Pearl mussel - The black thick-shelled river mussel with a curved periphery.
(**Mya margaritifera** Linnaeus & Muller) Tab. IV fig. 1.

If, as I have already remarked, other freshwater mussels produce pearls, and if, as according to the new observations of Chemnitz and Linnaeus, all mussels can produce pearls, then this mussel still deserves the name of 'pearl mussel', as it produces the most pearls of all the river mussels. I place it amongst the mussels with a toothed-hinge with some certainty, as it has this single tooth. I must remark, that when I speak of the tooth, I am speaking of one shell only. I do not mean the opposite shell, which has other teeth or a hollow, into which the teeth of the first shell fit. This pearl mussel has basically only the one tooth. The hollow in the opposite shell has two projections, which various writers have compared to teeth, and thus described the mussel as having three teeth. The tooth, of which I speak, is called by Linnaeus "Dentum primarium'.

Of all the river mussels, this is the most attractive and it possesses the strongest shell. This shell is black or dark brown, and it cannot be made more beautiful by artists. It is cracked and flaking, like the shell of an oyster. My largest example is from the R. Elster, and it is five and one quarter zoll broad, two and three quarters zoll long and one and a half zoll deep. I possess one nearly as large from Franconia, and a smaller example from Celle. I do not doubt that larger and smaller examples can be found.

The hinge is rather strong, horny, shiny and a little opaque. The side edge is open on both sides, on one more so than the other. The shell is bulging in the middle. This is similar to the 'large duck-bill', but the pearl mussel can be distinguished by its stronger shell and toothed hinge. The shell is almost eaten through by worms, more so than a sea mussel, or any of the other river mussels.

All the writers describe this mussel as being black or dark-brown except Klein who describes them as yellowish green.

What beauties this mussel lacks outside, nature has given it plenty inside. No river mussel has such a fine mother-of-pearl, which resembles that of a sea mussel, as this one. The edge of the mother-of-pearl is bordered by a brown band, and this is probably the last deposits made by the animal in making the shell grow. On younger examples this band is not visible. The entire remaining part of the shell has an uncommonly beautiful mother-of-pearl, which is of such quality, that pearls may be turned from the tooth. These, however, do not have the value of normal pearls.

The area where the animal attaches itself to the shell with fine nerves, is noticeably deepened, shiny, and striped with twisted furrows. The one near the hinge is smaller than on the other end. The tooth is uniformly strong, with 1, 2, or 3 indentations, although these are not deep. There are a corresponding number of projections in the hollow in the opposite shell. Of all the pearl mussels which I possess and which I have

seen, the example from Celle has the most pointed
tooth. On the vast majority, the hollow into which the
tooth fits has two pointed projections but this mussel
from Celle has only one. That various writers reckon
these projections to be teeth, I have already remarked.
These 'side teeth' catch hold of depressions on the main
tooth, as Herr D. Martini has already observed. Herr
Muller has not however observed this on his specimens.

In his description Schroeter not only refers to
the presence of more than one layer which forms the
shell, but also to the eighteenth century practice of
turning the shell tooth to produce 'pearls'. These are
readily recognised by their horizontal banded
structure. This also applies to modern turned pearl
nuclei, produced from the United States freshwater
mussel shells, which form the basis of the Japanese
marine cultured Mikimoto Pearls.

The freshwater pearl mussel has a bivalve
shell and is classified by zoologists as belonging the
the phylum MOLLUSCA. All living things are divided
into two major groups: Plants and Animals; which
are themselves subdivided into major sections.
Animals are also divided into two main groups :
animals which possess a backbone, the Vertebrates
(e.g. fish, birds, mammals, etc.). and animals without
a backbone, the Invertebrates (e.g. corals, jellyfish,
insects, etc.). These are further divided into major
groups known as phyla, the divisions being based on
the presence or absence of common features, (e.g.
jointed legs, shell, etc.).

In the case of the pearl mussel, the absence of
a backbone means that it belongs to the Invertebrates,
whilst the additional features of having an
unsegmented body, together with the possession of a
calcareous shell, places it into the phylum Mollusca.

The molluscan shell, which forms the exoskeleton
of the majority of molluscs, is directly responsible for
the production of pearls. It principally consists of

carbonate of lime, in the form of calcite or aragonite, and is normally three layered. In some molluscs, (for example, garden slugs), the shell has been greatly reduced and may be entirely absent. B. B. Woodward outlines the structure of a shell in his *The Life of the Mollusca* published in 1913, as follows:

The shell is mainly composed of carbonate of lime, as much as 95 per cent., in the form of calcite or aragonite, being often present, with the admixture of a chitinous substance, "conchyolin"; a little phosphate of lime and a trace of carbonate of magnesium are also present. It originates in a shell-gland, or pit, in the embryo, and the successive layers of which it is built up are formed by additions to the margin, and are deposited in order from the outermost to the inner one by a series of special cells situated in the thickened margin of the mantle. The outermost layer, or "periostracum", [the term "epidermis", which has been extensively mis-applied to this layer, should be reserved exclusively for the outer layer of the skin of the animal itself.], contains the greatest abundance of chitine-like material in its composition, and is the work of cells at the very edge of the mantle. Its function is to protect the underlying layers from the secretion of acid in water, or from that of the weather on land. It varies greatly in appearance, being sometimes smooth and shiny, at others, rough and coarse; frequently it is fibrous. In many forms it readily rubs off; in others it is firmly united to the true shell beneath. The second, or principal layer, usually forms the greater thickness of the shell proper, or *'ostracum'*, and is secreted by cells farther from the mantle margin; it may be coloured, and is often made up of prisms of calcite, as in **Pinna**, though it frequently has a porcelaineous structure. The cells more remote from the mantle edge deposit the innermost layer of the ostracum, thus thickening and strengthening the shell. This layer (*'nacreous* *layer'*) is of aragonite, and frequently formed with overlapping plates, thus giving rise to the iridescent appearance known as Mother-of-Pearl. The remaining surface of the mantle also secretes shelly matter on occasion, either for the purpose of further strengthening the shell, or repairing an injury remote from the edge, or of filling up unoccupied spaces; and in most Mollusca this deposit differs in structure from that of the other layers. In the pearl-producing shells, however, such as the Top Shells (Turbinidae and Trochidae), the Pearl Oyster (**Meleagrina**), and many freshwater mussels (**Unio, Anodonta**, etc), as well as **Nautilus**, this last form of shelly secretion is not differentiated from the nacreous layer, and is very abundant. In the case of the Pearl Oyster and freshwater mussels, foreign bodies introduced accidentally or intentionally between the mantle of the animal and the shell become coated with pearl. In this way *'Blister Pearls'*, and occasionally detached pearls, are formed; but the true pearl of commerce, as will be seen later, is developed within in the tissues of the animal.

MOLLUSCAN NOMENCLATURE
& CLASSIFICATION

Before progressing to discuss the pearl mussel in more detail, it may be useful to outline briefly the principles of molluscan classification and the establishment of a latinised scientific name.

The phylum Mollusca is itself subdivided into six major groups known as Classes, these being:

1. Class Gastropoda.

This Class contains over three-quarters of living molluscs and is characterised by having a soft body and large foot, which is normally enclosed in a hard, protective, usually coiled shell. The majority are active, highly mobile, and occur in the sea, on land and in freshwater. There are about thirty thousand described species including marine forms such as Limpets, Top Shells, Cowries, Cones, and Volutes.

2. Class Cephalopoda.

Cephalopods are a highly evolved group of marine molluscs which possess a well-developed head with eyes and a ring of normally eight or ten sucker-bearing arms or tentacles. The mouth has a horny, beak-like structure which is used for tearing their prey, since all living species are carnivores. Some, such as the Pearly Nautilus, have an external shell, but in the majority the shell is reduced and internal, or entirely absent. The class includes the octopus and squids as well as the Pearly and Paper Nautilus.

3. Class Scaphopoda.

The Class of Scaphopoda, commonly known as Tusk Shells, contains over a thousand species, and is considered by some as being the most primitive group of Mollusca. All are marine and have a tubular shell, which is open at both ends. In life the narrower posterior end of the shell protrudes above the sand in which the animal lives. There is no distinct head, eyes or gills, but the foot is large and there is a well-developed radula. Tusk Shells feed mainly on protozoa and other microscopic organisms.

4. Class Polyplacophora.

This Class, also known as Amphineura, contains the Chitons or Coat-of-Mail Shells, whose strange segmented shells of eight plates held together by a leathery band or girdle resemble woodlice when curling up for protection. All are marine and possess a well-developed radula, being mainly vegetarians. They have a large foot, but lack tentacles. There are about a thousand living species.

5. Class Monoplacophora.

This Class was only known from fossil forms until the middle of this century, when examples of living representatives were obtained by Norwegian research ships from deep water. Since then, further material of these primitive limpet-like shells, with their paired muscles and segmented body parts, has been collected which indicates that they may be highly spcialised rather than primitive. They are unlikely to be present in amateur collections due to the great depths at which they live.

And lastly, the group to which the pearl mussel belongs, namely

6. Class Bivalvia.

The Bivalvia shell is composed of two pieces, or valves, which are connected together by a hinge and an elastic-like structure known as the ligament. The majority have a large muscular foot, a pair of siphons and large mantle lobes which are responsible for secreting the shell. Most are sessile, (that is, permanently attached to the substrate in one place), although some, e.g. scallops, may move by rapidly opening and closing the shell valves. There are about ten thousand living species, which are restricted to the seas and freshwater ponds and rivers. Bivalves include oysters, mussels, cockles and tellins, and are the chief producers of pearls.

Having separated a mollusc into its appropriate Class, in the case of the pearl mussel, which has two valves hence belonging to the Class Bivalvia, it is then possible to classify it further into Subclass, Order, Superfamily, Family, Subfamily, Genus and finally species, the divisions being based on the relationships of a combination of shell and animal characters. A species name is unique to the particular animal in question and is based on the binomial system devised by the Swedish naturalist Carl Linnaeus in the 10th edition of his *Systema Naturae*, published in 1758.

In this binomial system there are two latinised names, the first or generic name denotes the group to which this animal and its close relatives belong and is started with a capital letter, which in the case of the pearl mussel is **Margaritifera**, whilst the second or specific name begins with a lower case and denotes the particular animal group in this genus, in this case again being **margaritifera**. This two part latinised name is followed by the name of the author who first described it, together with the date of publication. This combination of latinised Generic and specific second names, together with author and year of publication, is referred to as the species name and is unique to the animal concerned. This unique latinised name means that the species can be immediately recognised and identified by anyone, anywhere in the world. This is in contrast to the common English name, pearl mussel, which would not be identifiable by someone in France, Russia, Japan, Nova Scotia or North America, in all of which our pearl mussel lives.

In the present case the binomial name for the freshwater pearl mussel is:

Margaritifera margaritifera (Linnaeus 1758).

The reason the name of the author and year of publication are enclosed in brackets is that Linnaeus did not describe the **margaritifera** in **Margaritifera**, but in some other Genus. Later research has necessitated either a further division of Linnaeus's Genus into several Genera, or removal of **edule** to another genus. In this case Linnaeus described **margaritifera** as belonging to his genus **Mya**.

It should also be noted that Linnaeus is sometimes written as Linne (a name attributed to himself after receiving a knighthood).

Within the phylum Mollusca, **Margaritifera margaritifera** (Linnaeus 1758) is classified as follows:

Phylum	MOLLUSCA
Class	Bivalvia
Subclass	Heterodonta
Order	Unionoida
Superfamily	Unionoidea
Family	Margaritiferidae
Subfamily	Margaritiferinae
Genus	**Margaritifera**
Species	**margaritifera**
Date published	1758

Basic bivalve features are shown by the painters mussel, **Unio pictorum** (Linnaeus 1758), a distant relative of **Margaritifera margaritifera** which occurs in European freshwater rivers and lakes, including those of England and Wales, but which is absent from Scotland. The shell valves, which vary considerably in shape, thickness and sculpture from species to species, are united along their dorsal surface by an elastic ligament, which causes the valves to open. To offset this, the valves are held together by strongly developed muscles which are inserted onto the inner shell surface, producing characteristic muscle scars. These features, together with the dorsal hinge-plate, with or without interlocking tooth-like projections, are used as a basis for classification.

The animal's head is reduced and not visible outside the shell, the animal feeding by trapping organic particles as they pass over its large gills, having been drawn into the mantle cavity inside the shell valves via the inhalent siphonal aperture as a result of ciliary action. The foot, which is responsible for locomotion, is often large, protruding anteriorly between the shell valves. In young juveniles immediately following release from the fish host on completion of the parasitic glochidial state, the foot has a byssal gland which produces a silky thread, which assists in attaching the animal to the substrate, thus preventing it being washed downstream and ultimately into the sea. The right and left mantle lobes of the animal line the inner surface of the shell valves and are responsible for shell deposition, which normally occurs at the shell margins. If the animal is injured, however, the mantle lobes secrete a mucilaginous substance, which results in the closure of the damaged area and deposition of shelly matter. These mantle lobes normally fuse together at their posterior end to produce distinct inhalent and exhalent siphonal apertures. In the case of **Margaritifera margaritifera** however, this fusion is incomplete; the siphonal apertures being produced by the close apposition of the mantle lobes, which have well developed tree-like papillae which interlock together.

As in most bivalves, the sexes are separate, but the eggs are retained in specialised modified chambers of the gills, known as marsupia, whilst sperm are liberated into the surrounding water via the exhalent siphonal aperture and subsequently sucked in by the inhalent current of an egg-bearing female to fertilise the eggs in the marsupium. Here the fertilised eggs develop into free-swimming larvae, known as glochidia, which are subsequently released into the surrounding water via the female's exhalent siphonal aperture.

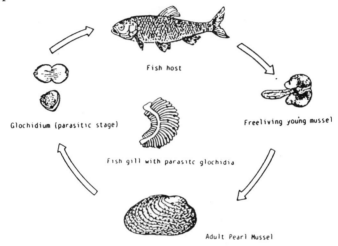

Fish host

Glochidium (parasitic stage)

Freeliving young mussel

Fish gill with parasitc glochidia

Adult Pearl Mussel

The freshwater pearl mussel, **Margaritifera margaritifera**, in common with other pearly freshwater mussels, has modified the typical marine bivalve free-swimming larval stage, presumably as a consequence of inhabiting freshwater. The mature mussel produces fertilised eggs in the autumn, which are retained in modified portions of the gills [=marsupia] until the following spring/summer. Here they develop into a bivalved larval stage known as a glochidium. These are liberated the following June-September and are capable of weak swimming movements. On coming into contact with a suitable fish host, normally a salmon or trout, they attach themselves to the fish's gills, causing an irritation to the fish tissues which grow around each glochidium to form a cyst. Here the glochidium undergoes a transformation of its tissues to develop into a baby mussel, during which time it obtains its nourishment from the fish host. This encystment lasts until late autumn or the following summer, the young mussels being liberated by the breakdown of the gill tissues, with the result that the juvenile mussels drop to the river bed, to assume a typical mussel lifestyle. Here they grow to adulthood, **Margaritifera** becoming mature at about twenty years and normally living to around eighty years in Britain. Populations up to one hundred and fifty years old are recorded from some continental localities.

This specialised life-cycle, involving fish parasitism, is unique to freshwater mussels and has arisen in order for the group to remain in freshwater, since the normal free-swimming veliger larva, characteristic of marine bivalves, would be washed back down into the sea by river currents. In the case of **Margaritifera**, the animal has evolved in association with salmonids, in this way ensuring its survival, since its parasitic glochidial stage infests small trout and salmon parr in July till September. This corresponds with the autumn run of salmon returning to their breeding grounds in the gravels of the river headwaters. As mature female salmon return upstream from the sea, the small salmon parr and trout become infected by released mussel glochidia and tend to follow the ripe female salmon upstream; precocious males in particular. After the female has shed her eggs she normally dies, but the infected salmon parr and small trout tend to remain for a time in the headwaters, during which time the parasitic glochidial stages of the mussel undergo metamorphosis and are liberated to the stream gravels. As time goes by they tend to get washed back downstream when the river is in spate, to recolonise and maintain the mussel population in the middle and lower reaches of the river.

HABITAT
OF FRESHWATER PEARL MUSSELS.

A. E. Ellis describes the general habitat for the pearl mussel in 1947 in his *Freshwater Bivavles* thus:

'In England **Margaritifera margaritifera** occurs only to the north and west of a line from Scarborough to Beer Head. ...It lives in the R. Exe, and passing thence east and north along the coast its next locus is the Whitby Esk in Yorkshire: travelling the other way it is found in Cornwall, all up the west coast and generally in Scotland north of Stirling, in Shetland, Lewis, Isle of Man and generally in Ireland, except the central limestone plain and the Shannon basin. It is absent from the whole of the midlands and south-east England. A typical locus is a quick running river up to 3 or 4 ft. deep with a mixture of boulders, stones and sand which accumulates behind large stones: it also lives in the Lakes (e.g. Loch Earn) through which such rivers flow. Most of its habitats are places in which fishermen would expect to get trout and hope for salmon, though it occasionally occurs in meagre streams. ...The great majority of its habitats contain soft water. The hardest water in which it occurs is the River Usk, Monmouth (51 milligrammes of calcium per litre). Boycott found that specimens from the River Wye 'lived happily in various hard waters with calcium 50-130 and finally in the Herts. Colne (Ca about 100) for several months'.

The fact that the pearl mussel appears to be absent from hard water habitats may be due to the lack of suitable hosts of its glochidial parasitic stage, i.e. trout or salmon parr, coupled with the increased phosphates present in these waters as a result of intensive agricultural practices over a period of several centuries. The other fallacy, that pearl mussels require rapidly flowing waters rich in oxygen, is also erroneous. In the past, I, myself, have kept examples in a sweet jar for periods in excess of two years, with the only attention of topping up the water levels with water from the local River Irvine. The mussels concerned appeared quite healthy and increased in size without any apparent problems through lack of oxygen. I would suggest that the mussel can survive such habitats, but is unable to breed due to the absence of suitable host fish for its glochidial stages, (trout and salmon parr), which require well aerated waters.

These observations are supported by nineteenth century records for this species in some man-made canals, thus J. G. Jeffreys writes in his 1862 *British Conchology*:

> It is found in several parts of the Swansea Canal where the bottom is gravelly, having been carried in by the watercourses which supply it.

This record was substantiated by J. Davy Dean and A. E. Boycott in 1928, with the discovery of a specimen in the National Museum of Wales at Cardiff, registration number 16.174 and labelled 'Swansea'.

N. Peace is also believed to have attempted to introduce pearl mussels which he had collected at Conway, North Wales, into the Sankey Canal at Warrington about 1866. A specimen in the R. D. Derbishire Collection, Manchester Museum, bears a label *Warrington, Sankey Canal, Peace, 1866*. Derbishire wrote about this specimen to J. W. Taylor in 1891:

> Sankey Canal, Warrington, I have heard of this locality years ago, but I recently got amongst some shells, both land and freshwater, of a deceased friend and collector one fine one, with his label - 'N. Peace, Sankey C. Warrn. 1866', which is now as valuable as the canal is, I am told, poisoned with chemicals. The specimen is of the form with a slightly

arcuated ventral line, very moderately eroded and in perfect condition.

A. E. Boycott records in the *Yorkshire Weekly Post* for the 10th July 1920:

Unio margaritifer is confined to waters or rivers poor in calcic substances, and is quite absent from the eastern counties of England, where calcareous oolites and chalk give rise to hard water. Mr. W. West of Bradford kept specimens alive for 2 years in Bradford tap-water, and found that "hard" water killed the creatures immediately.

There is a previous captive record by Friedel, published at Frankfurt in 1878 in the Zoologische Garten, volume 19, which claims that specimens of **Unio margaritifera** (Linnaeus) had been kept alive in the Aquarium at Dublin since April 1872, a period of just over six years.

Not all attempts at introducing pearl mussels proved successful, however, as evidenced by the following note on the Mollusca of Croydon by K. McKean in the *Transactions of the Croydon Natural History and Scientific Society* for 1882 -3:

I made an attempt to introduce it into the Croydon District seven years ago. One hundred and fifty specimens were sent from the River Don, Aberdeenshire and deposited in July 1875 in what appeared to be a suitable location in the Wandle, between Bridge House, Wallington and Hackbridge. The mussels though packed in wet moss were rather languid when put into the river. The sickly ones were immediately attacked by leeches; fifty-two dead shells were taken within a week. None seem to have survived long. The lower part of the Don where the mussels live contains 5.8 grams inorganic matter per gallon, whereas the Wandle holds 19 grams inorganic matter per gallon. The Don has 2.5 grams organic (vegetable) matter per gallon and the Wandle 1.74.

It is also worthy of note that on numerous occasions pearl mussels have been successfully introduced into suitable rivers, thus, L. M. Pratten writes in the *Naturalist* for 1864:

At Braystones on the Irt, a tributary of the Calder, in large quantities, where I have frequently seen them protruding their short siphons out of the mud on a hot sunny day. Tradition says that these shells were introduced here by a former owner, Sir John Hawkins, who had a patent for fishing them.

In The *Scottish Naturalist* for 1885, W. Japp records introducing them into the River Isla:

I have sometimes wondered why the black pearl mussel (**Unio margaritiferus** Turton, **Alasmodonta margaritiferus** Gray), is not to be found in the bed of the Isla from its rise in the Forest of Caenlochan, at the head of Glenisla, Forfarshire, down to the confluence of the Isla and the Dean, a distance of about 18 miles. The reason may be found in the fact that the bed of the river for this distance is stony; the river is usually rapid, and there is an absence of smooth and slow-moving water, which with a gravelly bottom, forms the best habitat of the Pearl Mussel.

He continues:

A colony of 3,000 mussels was planted on 15th October 1881 in the Isla at a point well up the river, where the channel is full and comparatively deep. They were brought from the Balquhidder River in Rob Roy's country to a place called Nyds in the parish of Glenisla. The place selected is a convenient bend in the River Isla which forming a right angle, has gathered an alluvial deposit, in which I hope they will thrive.

In the same article he makes the following observations:

The favourite habitat is smooth and slow moving water, with a gravelly bottom.

There are thousands in a sluggish piece of water of considerable extent in Balquhidder River, the average depth of which is about 7 feet.

If by any chance the trunk of a tree becomes fixed across the bed of the stream, so as to act like a croy, making the current less rapid, mussels will soon occupy this sheltered spot and will at once burrow a couple of inches into the gravel and adapt themselves to the requirements of their surroundings. There are all kinds and conditions of river beds and mussels soon find out and take possession of the most eligible sites.

If the shell is standing on its end, a little open at the top, it is a sign of life and energy. It is not certain that they hear; but they are very sensitive to the effect of light and touch; but by the latter expression I do not mean direct contact, but the result say of impact, caused by a stone falling in the bottom, or by a stick suddenly striking the bed of the stream. They are exceedingly acute in sight; if a boat passes over at a scarcely perceptible pace, these molluscs at once close their shells, so as in an instant to give evidence that they not only saw but feared an enemy.

Their natural preference is to burrow and it has been found that where a piece of water has been almost depopulated by too severe fishing, very soon a new colony may be seen taking up the position and studding the bottom of the river in myriads. Such a gravelly bottom gives also the favourite feeding ground of the mollusc. Though at times obliged to take refuge in clay, on it they are much poorer and leaner than on gravel. They are able like trout to adapt themselves in colour to that of the bottom on which they live, so that if the clay is blue, the mussel becomes blue; and even the pearls in such mussels assume a bluish tint. They are very conservative in their location, and it is believed that if nothing disturbs them, they can be identified as occupying the same upright position for thirty years or more.

Vitality: Mr. Farquharson believes that they may reach quite a patriarchal age, and that they may even live hundreds of years. They have been found deep in the gravel, even in railway excavations, at a depth of 20 feet to which depth it has been supposed they have burrowed, though something must be allowed for subsequent deposition of sediment. Mr. Farquharson some years ago tried an experiment. He selected about 1,000 shells and from each of these chipped off a piece of the shell and replaced them in the stream. About 18 years after he found that these mussels had grown only one inch so they might still be said to be in their teens. On this calculation it would require 144 years to reach its full size, as the average length of a mature shell is 8 inches. A full grown mussel can protrude a couple of inches from the opening of its shell. When so protruded the eyes can be seen peeping out. It is sometimes difficult to haul the creature out of its burrow, but this difficulty is lessened when the burrow is in loose gravel. They are able to move from place to place, one may trace on the muddy river beds the zigzag marks left by them on their mysterious errands. In a mussel bed shells of all ages and sizes are brought up by the drag net, which is often used in fishing for them. Mr. Farquharson has examined myriads of mussels in a year, yet in all his long experience he has only found 2 or 3 dead ones, this goes to show that it is very long lived.

J. B. Doyle writing in the *Proceedings of the Natural History Society of Dublin* in 1863 states:

The habitat of the pearl mussel I have found almost invariably to be in deep pools of rivers, which flow through alluvial or marshy bottom sands. It is often extremely difficult to see in consequence of their shells being the same colour as the mud in which they are embedded.

J. Dixon writes on this species in the *Naturalist* for 1864:

It seems very susceptible to the action of light, for under the full blaze of a bright mid-day sun it emerges more out of the gravel and protruding a portion of its body through the partly opened valves is the more readily distinguished. If the sun becomes overcast, or the water above the shell be muddy it immediately closes. The country lads generally select a bright noonday to look for them and take them either by wading or by thrusting the end of a long slender rod into the half-open shell, which instantly closes on it. It loves to lurk in the shallow and quick running parts of the river, among gravel and small stones and burrow generally in a somewhat oblique position. Only a small portion of it is visible and this being black and not unfrequently covered with a little moss, requires a well practised eye to detect it among the surrounding stones, for one of which it may easily be mistaken.

H. Crowther writing on a colony in the Whitby Esk in *The Naturalist* for 1879 states:

In the Esk they abound mostly at about 2 feet from the sides, under bushes and in shallow water. The whole of the specimens were embedded in three fourths of their length in mud, sand and gravel. They are buried in an oblique position, having the anterior end buried, the ventral edge uppermost, with a gape of about three eighths of an inch, displays the edges of the mantle, and the posterior end well pointed up stream, the umbonal region when the shell reclines thus, must rest in the deepest stratum, which is apparent every time a specimen is withdrawn, to be black mud.

W. H. Heathcote, in a letter to J. W. Taylor, gives the following observations of a visit he had made to a colony in the River Lune on the 29th August 1887:

They were in what would be four feet of water at ordinary seasons, stuck in the mud, the posterior side up, under and around large stones, under one large shelving stone was a group of nine set so close together, that you could grasp them with the fingers all at once. In a space about 12 feet or so square was a colony of perhaps 200 (we got 13 dozen), the least I got was one and one eighth inches broad.

T. Ruddy wrote to J. W. Taylor in May 1887 the following:

I know of a very large colony of this shell in the River Dee at Llanderfell and I counted 165 in the colony but I feel sure there were more. They inhabit a quiet place, a sort of backwater from a strong stream. The bottom is gravelly and has a margin of large pebblestones.

The shells move about with the hinge or top horizontal and they leave an irregular furrow behind them one and a half inches wide. When they settle down they bury the anterior end in the gravel, or push it between the large pebbles. The shells are all eroded, and often have the **Ancylus** sticking to them and also plants of conferva. I cannot see any young shells. This is a puzzle to me. All the shells in the colony are from four to four and seven eighths inches from anterior to posterior end and two to two and a half inches from hinge to margin.

Further to T. Ruddy's observations on pearl mussel movement, A. E. Shipley states in an article 'On the Migration of the Mussel' in *Country Life* for the 7 March 1914 pp. 356-7 that the rate of progress of a mussel is five yards in twenty four hours which would mean the animal would move about one mile in a year.

The apparent lack of young mentioned by Ruddy and other early workers may be due to the secretive nature of newly liberated post parasitic juveniles which we believe may take up their existence buried beneath the surface in fine river gravel further up-stream from the main mussel colony. The suggestion that their absence is purely due to collecting technique is not proven, since the majority of early collectors, although unable to find **Margaritifera** of three or four millimetres, still managed to collect the other freshwater bivalves, such as **Pisidium**, whose sizes were in this range.

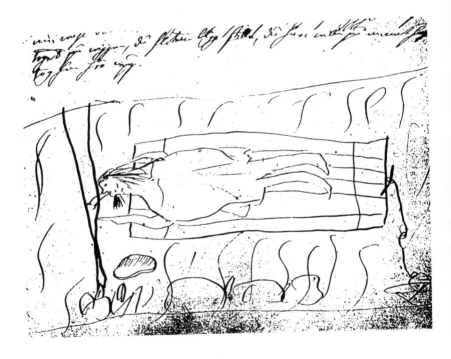

"Pearl fisher on a rock-anchored raft"
quill-and-ink sketch recently found in
Linnaeus' manuscripts.
(Linnaeus was a first-rate draughtsman;
this doodle has the air of on-the-spot
reporting about it).

METHODS FOR PEARL FISHING

Among the earliest accounts of pearl fishing in Scotland is that described in the following poem dating from about 1620 and published in 1638 by Henry Adamson in his *The Muses' Threnodie: or Mirthful Mournings on the death of Mr. Gall.*

This time our boat passing too nigh the land
The whirling stream did make her run on sand,
Aluis, we cried, but all in vain t'abide,
We were constrained, till flowing of the tide.
Then Master Gall, quod I, even for my blessing,
Now let us go, the pretious pearles a fishing,
Th'occasion serves us well, while here we stay
To catch these muscles, you call toyts, of Tay,
It's possible if no ill eye bewitch us
We jewels finde, for all our days t'enrich us...

...Content said Gall; then off our shoes we drew
And hose, and from us we our doublets threw,
Our shirt-sleeves wreathing up, without more speeches,
and high above our knees we pulling our breeches,
In waters go, then straight mine arms I reach
Unto the ground, whence cleverly I fetch
some of these living pearled shells, which do
Excell in touching and in tasteing too '
As all who search, do by experience try,
And we oftimes; therewith I loudlie cry.
Good master Gall, behold I found a pearle,
A jewel I assure you for an Earle.
Be silent, said good Gall, or speak at leisure,
For men will cut your throat to get your treasure...

A more refined method employed for obtaining pearls from freshwater pearl mussels was observed in the mid eighteenth century by Linnaeus, during his Lapland journey and described in his journal as follows:

At Purkijaur I hired a man to show me the manner of fishing for pearls, for which I agreed to pay him six dollars. He made a raft of five timbers as thick as my body, and two fathoms in length. At each end was a staple to which the anchor was attached. This anchor was nothing more than a stone, tied round with twigs of birch that it might not be lost, to which he fastened a cord, about two fathoms in length, made of birch twigs. He was likewise furnished with a pole of the same length, which served him to steer his raft, as it floated along the strong current. The bottom of the river is not easily seen at any great depth; but when he could distinctly perceive it, he dropped his stone anchor, fixing the upper end of the rope to the staple on the raft, by which it became stationary. Whenever he wished to examine another spot, he weighed anchor, and resigned himself to the force of the current. Where the water was shallow, he stood up-right on the raft; but where the depth was considerable, he lay at full length, with his face downwards, looking over the edge of the raft.

By means of a pair of wooden pincers, two fathoms in length, he laid hold of the pearl oysters (rather muscles, **Mya margaritifera**,) and drew them up. The part of the pincers below the joint or hinge was about a span long, and of three fingers breadth, hollowed out at the points, one of which was curved, the other flat. Taking the other end of these pincers in his hands, he easily directed them to the spot where he saw shells lying. The latter were generally open, so that they might readily be discerned by the whiteness of their inside; but when the water is very much agitated, the animals immediately close their shells, though destitute of eyes or ears.

The form of the shell is elliptic-oblong, with a contraction, or shallow notch as it were, about the middle of their outer margin. The man opened them by means of a whilk shell, which he thrust with violence between the valves, for it is impossible to effect this with the finger only. He introduced the point of the whilk in the centre of the base. or broader end, of the muscle,, searching for the pearls chiefly towards the other end, on the inside of the valve. If the inside of the latter be white, the pearl is white; but if dark or reddish, the pearl is of the same colour.

When it was first discovered that this neighbourhood produced pearls, the river at Purkijaur was the place where the principal pearl fishery was established. But now it is nearly exhausted. When the discovery of this bed of pearl muscles was first made, it is said the shells were in such abundance that nobody could reach the bottom of them, which is far from being the case at present.

There is no external sign about the shell, by which it is possible to know whether it contains a pearl or not. Consequently many thousands are destroyed to no purpose before one pearl is found. It is also a great pity that all the muscles are killed in consequence of this examination. Each pearl is either attached to the shell, or loose. They are found at all seasons of the year, and are sometimes thrown out of the shell spontaneously by its inhabitant.

Linnaeus' observations on the pearl fishers of Purkijaur differ little from those described by Schroeter, 1783 in his *Einleitung* concerning the pearl fisheries at Celle in Lower Saxony, Germany.

On the pearl mussels from Celle, I wish to repeat some of Her Taube's remarks. They are found in streams, but none are found in streams with rapid flowing water, and a hard, sandy or stony bed. In such streams, which in spring and autumn have rapid flowing water, and in the summer are mainly dry, one may seek pearl mussels in vain. The most pleasant time to fish for them is when the winter has lost some of its coldness, and is bearable to the pearl fisher. the fishers can be seen, with a bottle hanging around their neck, and carrying a stick, which is strong enough to support them, lest they fall. They fish in still water, against the stream, and generally in bright sunshine. The fishers believe that a mussel possessing pearls does not change its habitat, and if a mussel is found which is not easily removed from the stream bed, and possesses unusual features, such as a hollow, a furrow, a broad stripe of another colour, unnatural crookedness of both shells, or an unusual rounding, then the fishers believe it could contain a pearl. Whether it is ripe or not cannot be ascertained from external peculiarities. It is discerned from the known folds and lines on the shell, which the animal lays yearly. The pearl is separate from the flesh of the animal and must therefore grow with the shell. Seldom, however, is such a pearl usable. The unripe pearls are found to the left of the hinge, toward the broadest end. They sit under the skin of the so-called "'beard" of the mussel. Often, the pearl is found at the other end, sitting between the inner skins. Occasionally, two or more are found in one shell, although they are seldom all ripe and fine; very often they are all dull and useless. A pearl of 18 grammes, of fine form and ripeness is very rare in these waters, and would be a great treasure.

The Rev. James Robertson in 1794, writing on Callander Parish in *The Old Statistical Account of Scotland*, states:

Pearls:- In the Teith are found considerable quantities of muscles, which some years ago, afforded great profit to those who fished them, by the pearls they contained, which were sold at high prices. The pearls were esteemed in proportion to the glossy fineness of their lustre, their size and shape. Some of the country people made £100 in a season, by that employment. This lucrative fishery was soon exhausted; and it will require a considerable time before it can be resumed with profit, because none but the old shells, which are crooked in the shape of a new moon, produce pearls of any value.

Pearl Fishing:- They are fished with a kind of spear, consisting of a long shaft, and shod at the point with two iron spoons, having their mouths inverted; their handles are long and elastic, and joined at the extremity, which is formed into a socket, to receive the shaft. With this machine in his hand, by way of staff, the fisher, being often up to his chin in water, gropes with his feet for the muscles, which are fixed in the mud and sand by one end, presses down the iron spoons upon their point; so that by the spring in the handles, the open to receive the muscle, hold it fast, and pull it up to the surface of the water. He has a pouch or bag of network hanging by his side, to carry the muscles till he comes ashore, where they are opened. The operation is much easier in shallow water.

The Rev. G. Gordon describes a further method in his Mollusca of Morayshire in the *Zoologist* for 1854:

In several parts of the rivers Spey, Avon and Doveran, it has been gathered for the sake of the pearls - few and far between - expected to be found within it. Lachlan Shaw, the historian of Moray, 1775, says 'in the river Spey there are pearl shell in which I have seen many ripe pearls of a fine water and great value', Mr. Charles Grant, schoolmaster of the parish of Aberlour, has collected and kindly communicated the information, 'that about eight or ten years ago, an individual from Inverness fished for pearls at Abernethy, on the Spey, but, after the toil of two weeks and the destruction of many a mussel, he is reported to have carried off no greater reward than six or seven, of what size or value is unknown, as he was so tenacious of his fancied treasure, that he refused to exhibit them to the inspection of any one. He found the shells in still pools having a muddy bottom; and the instrument of landing was a long pole, having a string with a noose attached to its end. He contrived to get the noose round the shells, and tightening it, with a sudden jerk, drew them ashore'.

Mr. Grant adds 'In my fishing excursions I have frequently met with the shells, which are about four inches long by two broad, and of a dark gray colour outside; but I have no recollection of having ever seen one with a live fish. I strongly suspect that the flood of 1829 has destroyed great numbers of them, as their remains along the banks of the Spey are now less frequently to be met with than they were previous to that Period. There is a traditional account of an English Company having fished for them sixty or seventy years ago; but the fishing turned out unsuccessful and was discontinued. I have never seen or heard of any historical report of this company'.

David Dyson, writing on *The Land and Freshwater Shells of the Districts around Manchester* states:

In the Autumn of 1849 I visited the river Lune. At a place called Caton, about five miles above Lancaster, I found these shells in abundance. They can be seen from the banks of the river when the water is clear. They lie between the stones in the mud, with the ends pointing up. On taking a small stick and putting it between the valves, the animal will close the shell, and then it is easily lifted out of the water. But the better way is at once to go into the stream as this will save time. I stripped and entered, and by placing the eye near the surface saw the shells distinctly, and gathered them with ease.

J. B. Doyle in 1863 refers to Irish pearlfishers in the *Proceedings of the Natural History Society of Dublin* thus:

The favourite season is during summer months when the rivers are low. On a calm bright day the fisherman with a sharp pointed wattle and a large wooden scoop stations himself on the brink of a pool and waits until he sees some of the mussels moved, which they do with great rapidity by the aid of their strong muscular foot. Sometimes they lie basking, as it were, in the sunshine, the foot extended and mantle visible. The fisherman thrusts his pointed stick between the valves and lifts the shell out of the water - afterwards he wades into the pool and shovels them out wholesale onto the bank. The heap is then examined, the deformed and wrinkled shells are first examined as likely to contain the best pearls and then the remainder. At the extensive fisheries at Port Glerrone, Co. Antrim, on the Bann it was customary to throw the mussels into a large heap to decompose which they quickly do. They were then taken and washed in large tubs, the mass being stirred with a stick. After several washings the shells and grosser parts were removed and the pearls sought for at the bottom.

More recently W. Japp described the activities of the Angus pearl fisher John Farquharson in the Scottish Naturalist for April 1885:

John Farquharson, pearl fisher, Coupar-Angus, who dubs himself pearl-fisher to the Prince of Wales, and who certainly has been lucky in finding valuable pearls, and in selling the to the high-born. ..He has constructed for himself a small wherry the size of which is about 3 ft. 3 ins. each way. He seats himself in his little boat, and having provided himself with a long pole or wand, with a small split at the lower end, he eyes the mussels with correct aim; and when the bottom of the river is free from disturbance and the water peaceful and in its ordinary state, he can bring up about 6 mussels in a minute. He seizes the mussel with the split of the wand; and pushes it down until the swelling of the shell is passed, and with a gentle pull he renders the mussel a captive, and lands it in the wherry, or on the side of the stream.

The use of boats continued until fairly recently, but this method proves inefficient due to the difficulty of operating the cleft stick in deeper water. In addition, the process does not go down too well with other users of our rivers as indicated in the following note published in *The Field* on the 17th October 1908:

THE PEARL FISHERS OF THE TAY

Sir,

I should like to call the attention of the proprietors of the Tay to the great nuisance the pearl fisher has become to the salmon fisher. In summer, when the height of the river serves, it is no uncommon thing to find three and four pearl fishers in their primitive punts anchored in a beat, prodding about with their long cleft wands for the mussels, 'working' the pools and every inch of the river. They frighten what fish there happen to be in the pools, and, to increase the damage, they open the mussels and cast the shells back again into the river. These, with their bright, silvery inner surfaces shimmering in the stream, scare ascending fish and prevent them resting. Of course, beats with the best reputations for mussels and pearls suffer the most.

Besides the fishers with punts, there are others who wade; but the damage they do is comparatively small. The punt fisher is becoming more numerous, and asks no permission, as he used to do; he is of a very rough class, claims his 'fishing' as of right, and meets one's gillie's remonstrance with abuse and even threats. It is heartbreaking to find a beat that you had fondly hoped had had a nice rest occupied by the pearler puddling away for all he is worth, or to catch a glimpse of him dropping down into the next beat after completely spoiling your day's sport. On the Tay in the summer the angler's hopes should not soar too high, but with the demon pearler in full activity his prospect is grey indeed.

The reference to the pearl mussel shells being returned to the water frightening fish, is not the only problem produced by this action. In the majority of sites plundered by illegal amateur fishers, the animals have been indiscriminately killed by simply ripping the shell valves apart. The resulting broken shell and animal are then thrown back into the river or left to decompose on the bank, the resultant putrefaction increasing pollution of the river waters. The damage produced in this way is further compounded since the majority of the amateur pearl fishing activities tend to occur in the summer months, particularly July and August, when the water levels are at their lowest.

Hamish Muir outlined the techniques employed during the period of the 1914-1918 War in an article in *Country Life* describing pearl fishing on Scottish Lochs and Rivers. In this he relates how the Callander pearl fisher's stock in trade consisted of a long box-like contrivance, with a glass bottom for looking through the water, to locate the shells, and a long stick cleft at the end for gripping the shells; fishing being achieved by wading in shallow water. He continues:

A dry season is especially conducive to a good harvest; a case in point being the long dry summer of 1913 when a record number of pearls was found in the Teith and Loch Vennacher; a few years ago a pearl found in the Teith was sold to a jeweller for £25.

W. Harrison Hutton, in a paper to the Leeds Conchological Club in November 1917 on British pearls, states:

Fishing methods - in this country and in Scotland and Ireland the great hindrance to the success of pearl production is the destructive manner in which it is carried on: hundreds of tons of immature mollusks are destroyed and there is no close season: and if a few good pearls are found in a river it is fished to death. The fishermen sometimes use a dredge, but mostly wade where the water is shallow. Where deep they use a cleft stick to pick up the shells and sometimes go out in a boat and use a water telescope to locate the shells and beds. There are some expert fishermen in Scotland and Ireland who can often judge when a shell contains a pearl by its outward appearance. Not long ago as much as £200 worth of pearl were found by one fisherman in Scotland.

Significantly little has changed to this day in the methods employed by Scottish pearl fishers who operate using a combination of those described above. They operate by wading up to their waist whilst viewing the river bed through a glass bottomed bucket during which process any suitable pearl mussels observed are obtained by using an ash stick which is split at the operational end to act as a pincer. The mussels thus collected are then examined to determine if pearls are likely to be present and if not, returned immediately unharmed to the water in the area they originated from. Any shells suspected of bearing pearls, however, would be placed in the canvas collecting bag attached to the pearl fisher's waist, where it would remain, normally for a maximum of two hours, until such time as sufficient likely pearl-bearing shells had been obtained, or the pearl fisher needed a rest from the continuous strain of bending down against the fastly flowing river current. At this point he would return to the river bank in order to examine the individual mussels in detail.

In the past, the shell valves were prised apart using another shell, or a knife, as described by Linnaeus, such actions resulting in the unnecessary death of the animal concerned. This, over the years, has led to the dramatic decline of the freshwater pearl mussel throughout its former range, to such an extent that it is currently under serious threat of total extinction. Sadly, such irresponsible actions are completely unnecessary, as it is a relatively simple process to examine an animal and remove any pearls present without causing any serious injury. This is accomplished by using a pair of the opening tongs, which have been recently developed by the semi - professional pearl fishers as a direct result of their concern for the future survival of the freshwater pearl mussel and pearl

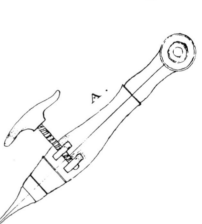

Opening Tongs drawn by Peter Gadd

fishing. These tongs consist of modified electricians' wire-strippers which can be inserted between the shell valves and opened, so that the valve margins are separated from one another up to a maximum of one centimetre. This enables the pearl fisher to examine the exposed mantle margins of the animal for the presence of pearls, these normally being found in the mantle lobes adjacent to the valve margins. Any pearls present can then be easily removed by the use

of a small stick without any serious injury to the animal. The opening tongs are then relaxed and the animal returned alive to the river bed, preferably as near to its point of origin as possible. Such released animals appear to be unaffected by such treatment and continue to live and reproduce quite happily, thus safeguarding the future pearl mussel colony. In addition, many pearl fishers tend to mark shells from which they have removed pearls, prior to returning the living mussels to the river, which helps reduce further disturbance of these individuals on subsequent pearl fishing expeditions.

Similar methods to those above were proposed during Linnaeus' time as exemplified by the patent by Peter Gadd for similar opening tongs which accompanied Linnaeus' evidence to the Swedish Secret Committee in relation to his claims for being able to produce cultured freshwater pearls.

Knowing whether a particular pearl mussel is likely to contain a pearl or not depends to a large degree on experience. Professional pearl fishers are in general relatively selective in the animals they collect to examine for the presence of pearls.

Schroeter writes on this aspect of the art as follows:

Can one judge from outside whether a pearl-mussel contains a pearl? This is certainly to be wished for, because it would prevent the unnecessary death of so many pearl-mussels. I believe that there is no sure way of telling, without any danger of error. In the meantime I will repeat a few distinguishing signs which sometimes prove that the mussel has pearls. .... Fissherstein describes the following [criteria]:- 1) when the mussel has five, six or seven longitudinal stripes, 2) when swellings are found on the sides, 3) when one side is crumpled near the narrow end, and 4) when there is a deep furrow on the shell. These hallmarks appertain more to mussels of the sea and of the large rivers near the sea, than to our river mussels. Jetse speaks of this fact with some confidence. I advise experienced and thinking readers not to dismiss his thoughts out of hand, when you have read them.

The first discoverer found the hallmarks after many tries. He remarks that when the pearl is ripe it is possible to dislodge the pearl from its position in the belly of the mussel and to move it downwards; when this occurs, a purple-red fluid seeps from the area from which the pearl was dislodged. Then one can clearly see, without opening the shell, whether there are pearls or not. This difference is not visible through external distinguishing marks, and must be noticed by experience.

The mussel - animal throws its shell off, and obtains a new one, which has been gradually growing under the old. The old becomes very brittle and flaky, resembling the layers of a slate quarry. During the time, until the new shell is ready, the pearl develops, and this is at its best size and ripeness when the new shell can be seen in certain places through the old. When mussels like this are found, which exhibit the before-mentioned distinguishing features, they can be opened, and a most beautiful pearl is found.

THE VALUE OF PEARLS

Schroeter writes:

The value of our inland pearls seems to be underestimated. When the size is taken into question, one must say, that the largest pearls are found in the sea, or in the large rivers near the sea. Only those of middle size and those of the size of a sugar-pea from the rivers match those from the sea. It is also noticeable that those from the rivers do not match the oriental pearls in size, lustre, or form. One must be on ones guard with respect to controversy over this question. We have found in our rivers, some pearls, which approach the oriental, and have had a similar worth and selling price. I must venture to say, that it is only prejudice which makes one say that the Indian pearls are always superior to ours, and that these must be more expensive. It is also prejudice, that we give much more value to foreign items than to our own, and I wager, that for all the foreign pearls, for which we must pay high prices, there are as many to be found in our rivers. Tavernier, the great jeweller, states that Bavarian pearls can be found with a value of a thousand guilden.

A note in *Science Gossip* for 1894 provides an idea of the relatively high values obtained at that time:

The pearlfishery in the north of Ireland has been fairly successful this season, several varying in value from £10 to £20 having been found, besides many smaller, in the river Strule, which is considered the best water in Ulster for these objects.

The following letter, dated 6 June 1894, in the *Irish Naturalist* adds:

In the past week a number of valuable pearls were found in the Strule between Omagh and

Newtonstewart. E. Mullan got one weighing 10 grains for which he refused £10. Thomas Short got six, all good colours and shapes. William Muldoon, nine pearls; J. Donnelly fourteen, four of which were perfection and very valuable. The Strule is the best river in Ulster for pearls.

This fishery continued into the twentieth century, as shown by the following note in the *Daily Mail* for the 28th July 1908:

Pearl fishing in Ulster:- During the past week some valuable finds of pearls have been made in the rivers round Strabane, County Tyrone. Pearl fishing is a regular employment in these streams, which are all tributaries of the Foyle, and for a considerable time past business in this line had been dull. A day or two ago, however, one man, after half an hour's fishing, found a pearl, which he disposed of to a local jeweller for £8. Several other smaller ones were found by the same person, and fetched from 10s. to 20s. Some amateurs have been successful in getting very fine gems.

A note in *The Evening Post* for 25th January 1913 reads:

PEARL FISHING IN SCOTLAND

It is not generally known that pearls are obtained from some of the rivers in Scotland, but this was once a flourishing industry, although of late it has become neglected. Of the most important pearl producing rivers, the Ythan, Aberdeenshire, is certainly one of the best known. This sluggish stream is said to have yielded the great pearl which was set in the crown of Scotland, and about 1750 a Mr. Tower, of Aberdeen, received £100 sterling from a London jeweller for a parcel of pearls from the Ythan. On the river Earn, a lovely tributary of the Tay, mussel gathering used to be quite a trade, and the pearls found were the means of subsistence for many families. No Scottish gems, indeed, are considered better than those procured now and again from the Teith. A splendid specimen which was found comparatively recently near its junction with the Forth, is at present in the possession of a Callander jeweller. Its weight is 35 grains, and it is valued at £100.

W. Harrison Hutton in his 1917 paper to the Leeds Conchological Club, writes:

Pearls of British origin are mentioned by Pliny, A.D. 23 - 79, whilst Origen, A.D. 185 - 253, described British pearls as next in value to those of India, stating they were of a rich golden colour, but less transparent. Robert Sibbald, physician to Charles II, records a necklace of Scotch pearls valued at 2,000 crowns. Great numbers have been obtained from the Doon and Don and in 1861 a German merchant established a great trade in Scotch pearls. Pearls have been and still are found in the Forth, Teith, Ythan, and Spey: in 1862 specimens were found ranging in value from 10 shillings to £2. 6s. 0d. each. Queen Victoria gave for a Scotch pearl, I believe from one of the above rivers, 40 guineas. The Duchess of Hamilton and the Empress Eugenie also purchase a number of Scotch pearls, and a necklace of them was sold in 1864 for £350. The value of Scotch pearls found in 1864 was over £12,000 and some of the choice ones fetched from £5 to £150 to £500 each. **Unio margaritifer** was the chief producer. In recent years the Tay, Earn, and Teith in Perthshire, the Dee, Don and Ythan, in Aberdeenshire, the Spey and Findhorn in Inverness-shire - also the Doon (of Burns), the Nith and Annan have all produced a fair amount of good pearls. The Tay pearls are not of a good class. Those of the Isla are usually fine. The Earn pearls are of a good class, though not very plentiful. In Ireland the river Bann produced, and still does so, some very good pearls, and in 1907-8 Lady Dudley presented Queen Alexandria with a number of pearls from Connemara.

British pearls are mostly inferior in colour and lustre, but a few have a fiery tint and great lustre: pink ones are sometimes found and are greatly prized, but the best have a pure white light. One found in Aberdeen not long ago sold for £50 at first sale, it was 1/17 inch in diameter and weighed 21 grains.

The French rivers produce a fair amount of good pearls for colour and size, and pearl shells are largely used in France for the manufacture of buttons.

The rivers of Bavaria, Saxony and Silesia also produce good ones and for the last 42 or 43 years have an annual average of 200 first class, 395 second class, and 3,091 third class pearls.

In the same paper W. Harrison Hutton also points out that the value of a pearl is the natural value of the gem with the exception of an added few shillings for drilling and setting. This is in contrast to diamonds and other gems, whose value is often more than doubled as a result of cutting and setting. However, it should be remembered that the considerable value of a pearl necklace or group of pearls is greatly increased by the difficulty of matching the pearls concerned in relation to colour, size gradation, etc. In 1910 a pearl valued at £2 would compare to another of about the same quality weighing 4 grains with a value of £8 or above, but these values will depend upon quality, colour, scarcity, etc.

Further to Hutton's reference to the French using the shells for button manufacture, Paton in his 1847 work on the Mollusca of the Vosges describes a further use:

This mulette, which produces pearls, was, under the Dukes of Lorraine, preserved with care by the fishing guards, on account of this precious ornament; we will not say a lower word; but today its elongated, narrow, sinuous and thick valves have a very modest employ which is not wanting in utility; this is to serve to the inhabitants of the beautiful valley of the Vologne as a scraper fit to cleanse the interior of the 'vases de foue' which are in use in the housekeeping.

By the mid nineteen twenties records of notable pearls were few and far between as a result of the continuing depletion of mussel stocks through over fishing, coupled with increasing agricultural pollution and alterations to river courses through land drainage, hydroelectric schemes, etc. However, occasional finds still occurred, as shown by the following report in *The Daily Mail* for the 26th of March 1928:

FRESH WATER PEARL

FIND IN A FRENCH RIVER

PURPLE HUE TINGED WITH GOLD

from our own correspondent

Paris, Saturday.

Several pearls from fresh-water pearl oysters, which are extremely rare and are found only in a few streams in the British Isles and in one or two mountain torrents in the Auvergne region of France, have been discovered in the little River Ance, in the Lozere department.

These fresh-water pearl oysters are easy to fish because they live in very shallow water.

M. Raphael Dubois, an inhabitant of Grandrieu, a village on the banks of the River Ance, has found in one of these oysters an oval-shaped pearl seven millimetres in diameter and weighing forty centigrammes and of a magnificent orient. This fresh-water pearl, which is purple-hued, is tinged with gold, a peculiarity which is explained by the fact that the streams of the region wash down quite considerable deposits of alluvial gold.

Jewel experts say that this fresh-water pearl is believed to be bigger than any yet found in the streams of England and Scotland.

The claims that the above French pearl is bigger than any found in the streams of England or Scotland is not entirely true since large freshwater pearls, reputedly form Scottish rivers, occur in Victorian jewellery, such as brooches, tie-pins, etc. It is fair to say, however, that the quality of pearls collected in the twentieth century tend to be poorer and considerably smaller than in previous years, so that one of the above quality is exceptional. This is possibly due to a combination of overfishing, coupled with the destruction of habitat as a result of industrialisation, pollution and changes in agricultural practices.

The suggestion that the unusual golden colour of this pearl is associated with the presence of alluvial gold in the streams concerned is completely erroneous, the colour being entirely due to the structure and arrangement of the prisms of aragonite which form the pearl.

Since 1928, the importance of freshwater pearls has continued to decline, partly due to the introduction of cultured Mikimoto pearls, and partly through reduced availability resulting from the continuing decline of pearl mussel populations worldwide. A few pearl fishers have continued to eke out a meagre existence at this ancient occupation, perhaps the last full-timer being the Scot, Bill Abernethy, who is still going strong in 1993. Bill quoted the values of Scottish pearls in 1982 as:

Most of them are fairly small, maybe one-and-a-half to three grains in weight. A pearl that size would be worth about £3 or £4. A good-sized pearl of 10 or 12 grains, with a good shape and good lustre is worth about £70. Maybe more. This may sound a reasonable return, but at the turn of the century my grandfather could have asked £60 for a pearl of that size and £60 was worth an awful lot more than £70 is now. But so long as I make a living, I'm not bothered.

Amongst Bill's more noteworthy finds is the Abernethy Pearl, better known as 'Little Willie', whose history we will come to shortly. 'Little Willie' weighed in at fourty-four grains: thus beating the 1928 French pearl by four grains!

By the 1990's prices have again risen, and John Lochtie, the manager of Cairncross, the Perth jewellers specialising in Scottish freshwater pearls, reckons a good specimen is worth £250 to £300; about the same or a little more expensive than marine oyster pearls.

HISTORICAL ASPECTS
OF SCOTTISH PEARL FISHING

The alliterative mediaeval poem, *The Pearl*, consisting of one hundred and one stanzas totalling 1210 lines is one of the earliest written references to pearls in Britain. The original, whose author is unknown, forms part of a faded manuscript (MS Cotton Nero Ax) which is now preserved in the Library at the British Museum in London. It is thought to date from the period 1360 to 1400 and is written in a local dialect which is believed to originate from the North West Midlands. It describes how an eminent jeweller loses the most perfect jewel he has ever owned by dropping it in his garden. He goes to sleep and dreams that he sees his young daughter, who died at the age of three, adorned with pearls in a religious procession. Much of the poem is taken up with a theological discussion between the poet and his daughter, who tells him not to grieve for her. He tries to reach her across a stream but awakens at this point. The image of the precious pearl without a blemish is constantly used in the structure of the poem, where emphatic lines are repeated to link stanza groups.

The significance of this work is not only its strong reference to oriental pearls being used in Britain but also its apparent place of origin, namely the Midlands. Such a reference implies the presence of jewellers in the Midlands area, who presumably utilised British freshwater pearls from Cornwall, Wales, Northern England and Scotland. This is of particular relevance because Birmingham maintains a high profile in this trade to the present day, producing the gold blanks to designs of the Perth Jewellers, Cairncross, for the production of their modern brooches, earrings, necklaces, etc,

incorporating Scottish-taken freshwater pearls.
The original manuscript reads:

THE PARL

Perle, plesaunte to prynces paye!
To clanly clos in golde so clere,
Oute of Oryent, I hardly saye,
Ne proved I never her precios pere,
So rounde, so reken in vche arraye,
So smal, so smoꝑe her sydez were,
Queresoeuer I jugged gemmez gaye,
I sette hyr sengely in syngure,
Allas, I leste hyr in on erbere -
ꝑurz gresse to grounde hit fro me yot!
I dewyne, fordolked of luv-daungere,
Of ꝑot ꝑrying perle wythouten spot.

Or, in a modern English translation:

A pearl, such as a prince would choose
to set neatly in gold,
an oriental pearl, certainly
I never saw its equal,
perfectly round from each aspect
with delicate smooth sides.
Time and again, considering jewels
would I select this singular pearl.
But I lost the pearl in a garden.
It rolled away beneath the grass,
leaving me felled by love's blow
from the living pearl unblemished.

In another poem in the same MS, *Cleanness* , the author again alludes to pearls:

Though not the costliest gem to buy,
the pearl is praised by all collectors,
and prized wholly for flawlessness.

No stone can match its gleam,
shining brightly and smoothed round
without flaw or mark; a real pearl.
Nor does it spoil with wearing,
even when old, if it stays in one piece.
Forgotten, perhaps it becomes dim
hidden in a lady's bower:
it may be carefully washed in wine
to release its perfection again.

(Modern translation)

John Spuel gives the following account on the value of Scottish pearls in his *An Accompt current betwext Scotland and England* (Edinburgh, 1705):

If a Scotch pearl be of a fine transparent colour, and perfectly round, and of any great bigness, it may be worth 15,20,30, 40 to 50 rix dollars: yea, I have given 100 rix dollars (£16 9s. 2d.) for one, but that is rarely to get such I have dealt in pearls these 40 years and more, and yet to this day I could never sell a necklace of fine Scots Pearl in Scotland, nor yet fine pendants, the generality seeking for Oriental Pearls, because farther fetched. At this very day I can show some of our own Scotch Pearls, as fine, more hard and transparent than any Oriental. It is true that an Oriental can be easier matched, because they are all of a yellow water, yet foreigners covet Scotch Pearls.

Linnaeus writing in 1761 states:

The Scotch, Norwegian and Swedish pearls, are certainly whiter than the oriental and retain also longer their brightness and lustre; the oriental pearls however form with us the greatest number in consequence of their size, abundance, clearness and the particular regularity of their shape. But they turn soon yellow, when they lose half of their value and the detriment to the country is therefore greater through them.

The eminent English naturalist and traveller, Thomas Pennant refers to them in his *Tour in Scotland of 1769,* and again in his subsequent *Tour in Scotland and voyage to Hebrides* of 1772. In this he describes the River Tay in the neighbourhood of Perth:

July 27. There has been in these parts a very great fishery of pearl, got out of the fresh-water muscles. From the year 1761 to 1764, £10,000 worth were sent to London, and sold from 10s. to £1.16s. per ounce. I was told that a pearl had been taken there that weighed 33 grains; but this fishery is at present exhausted, from the avarice of the undertakers; it once existed as far as Lough Tay.

Further on in his journey he writes, having just left Aberdeen:

Aug. 9. Continue my journey: pass over the Bridge of Don; a fine gothic arch flung over that fine river, from one rock to the other: ride for some miles on the sea sands; pass through Newburgh, a small village, and at low water ford the Ythan, a river productive of the pearl muscle... Muscles are also much used for bait, and many boat loads are brought for that purpose from the mouth of the Ythan.

It is not certain whether these 'Muscles' refer to the edible marine mussel, **Mytilus**, or to the pearl mussel, **Margaritifera**.

The following reference to pearl fishing on the White Cart in Renfrewshire, near Paisley and Glasgow, is given in 1782 on Page 2 of Part 2 of *The history of the Shire of Renfrew* by George Crawford, continued by William Semple.

White Cart hath its source betwixt Eaglesham in this shire, and Evandale and Kilbride in Clydesdale: Its course for some miles, is northward, till at the castle of Cathcart (within two miles of the city of Glasgow)

it turneth north-west to Paisley, and from thence
northward to the kirk of Inchinnan.... a little below
that church. In this river of White Cart, a little
above the town of Paisley, there are found pearls so
fine and big, that they may compare with many
oriental, and have been taken notice of by some of the
most famous jewellers in Europe: They are found in the
ground of the river among the sand, in a shell larger
than that of a musk: The proper season of fishing them
is in the summer.

Sadly there is no evidence of mussels in this
river now, their demise being due to pollution
resulting from a combination of changes in agricultural
practice together with the effects of industrial
development.

In the 1796 *Old Statistical Account of Scotland*
the Reverend Robert Thomas writes in volume 18
concerning the Parish of Scone:

The Tay also abounds in the pearl-oyster. Numbers
of pearls were fished out of it about thirty-five years
ago.

According to Tytlers *History of Scotland,* trade
in Scottish pearls took place as far back as the 12th
century and a fishery existed up to 1800 on the River
Tay.

The Rev E. I. Burrow writes in his *Elements of
Conchology* of 1825:

Mya margaritifera, a species which is found chiefly
in the rivers of northern latitudes, is known to produce
pearls, partial secretions of the same matter which
forms the inner coating of the shell, in considerable
abundance. The British islands, especially Ireland,
have been considered famous for their fisheries of the
Mya, and a few pearls of great value have at different
periods been obtained from these sources; but the
quality of British specimens in general is by no means
held in the highest estimation.

John Stark, writing in his *Elements of Natural History*, published in 1828 states:

Unio elongata Lam. (**Mya margaritifera** Lin)

This species often produces pearls of considerable size and value. The mountainous rivers of Scotland are periodically fished for the purpose of procuring them; and it is said that the pearls in the Scottish crown are chiefly native ones, from the river Tay.

The celebrated Aberdeen naturalist, William McGillivray, writes in the 1843 edition of his **History of the Molluscous Animals of Aberdeenshire:**

The species reside in mud or gravel, in rivers.

It varies much in size, form, and colour. Young individuals are ovato-oblong, or ovate, with the epidermis olivaceous. Middle-aged individuals are of nearly the same form, but longer in proportion to their height, with the valves thick, the umbones decorticated or corroded, the epidermis dark -brown. In old individuals, some of which are from five to six inches in length, the lower margin is widely sinuate, so as to give the shell a curved appearance. The valves are very thick in old shells, their interior pearly, bluish or sometimes tinged with red, the epidermis nearly black. Pearls of various sizes, forms and colours are found in this species: spherical, hemispherical, binate, roundish, oblong; from a twelfth or less to half an inch in diameter; white, bluish, pink or dusky.

Common in the Dee, the Don, the Ythan, the Ugie, and the Doveran, in muddy and gravelly places.

William Leach, who died in 1836, wrote in his *A Synopsis of the Mollusca of great Britain arranged according to their natural affinites and anatomical structure* (1852):

This species in common with its exotic congeners produces excellent pearls, which are often sent to

India, and re-imported as Oriental pearls. There was formerly a pearl fishery in the Tay and there is one at present in North Wales, which is said to produce a very considerable revenue to the proprietor, who I have been told is a female.

Leach dedicated the above work to Savigny, Cuvier and Poli. The final version was edited posthumously by Leach's protege J. E. Gray, Keeper of Zoology at the British Museum, and published in 1852. Although only pp 1-116 and the plates were in type, some copies were circulated as early as 1820. Leach was formerly Assistant Keeper of Natural History at the British Museum until his forced retirement through ill-health in 1821.

Another Scottish naturalist and celebrity of this time, Hugh Miller of *Old Red Sandstone* fame, writes in his *My Schools and Schoolmasters* (1854) concerning his pearl fishing exploits in the River Conan, near Conan House, as follows:

When the river was low, I used to wade into its ford in quest of its pearl muscles (**Unio Margaritiferas**); and though not very successful in my pearl fishing, it was at least something to see how thickly the individuals of this greatest of British freshwater molluscs lay scattered among the pebbles of the fords, or to mark them creeping slowly along the bottom - when, in consequence of prolonged droughts, the current had so moderated that they were in no danger of having been swept away - each on its large white foot, with its valves elevated over its back, like the carapace of some tall tortoise. I found occasion at this time to conclude, that the **Unio** of our river fords secretes pearls so much more frequently than the **Unionidae** and **Anadonta** of our still pools and lakes, not from any specific peculiarity in the constitution of the creature, but from the effects of the habitat which it is its nature to choose. It receives in the fords and shallows of a rapid river many a rough blow from the sticks and pebbles carried down in times of flood, and occasionally from the feet of the men and animals that cross the stream during droughts; and the blows induce the morbid secretions of which pearls are the result. There seems to exist no inherent cause why **Anadon Cygnea**, with its beautiful silvery nacre - as bright often, and always more delicate than that of **Unio Margaritiferus** - should not be as equally productive of pearls; but, secure from violence in its still pools and lakes, and unexposed to the circumstances that provoke abnormal secretions, it does not produce a single pearl for every hundred that are ripened into value and beauty by the exposed current-tossed **Unionidae** of our rapid mountain rivers. Would that hardship and suffering bore always in a creature of a greatly higher family similar results, and that the hard buffets dealt him by fortune in the rough stream of life could be transmuted, by some blessed internal predisposition of his nature, into pearls of great price.

In 1867 M. S. Lovell notes in his *The Edible Molluscs of Great Britain and Ireland* :

Our Scotch pearl-fishery has, within the last few years, been most successfully revived; and in 1860 Mr. Moritz Unger, a foreigner, on making a tour through the districts where the pearl mussel abounds, found that the pearl-fishing was not altogether forgotten, many of the people having pearls in their possession, of which they did not know the value. He purchased all he could obtain; consequently, in the following year, many persons devoted their spare time to pearl-fishing , and during the summer months made as much as £8 to £10 weekly. The summer of 1862 was the most favourable for fishing, owing to the dryness of the season, and the average price was from £2. 6s to 10s., £5 being a high price. They now fetch prices varying from £5 to £20. The Queen purchased one Scotch pearl for 40 guineas; others a t high prices have been bought by the Empress of the French and the Duchess of Hamilton; and Mr. Unger has a necklace of these pearls valued at £350.* Pearl mussels are found in Lochs Earn, Tay, Rannoch, and Lubnaig, and in the Don, the Leith, and in many of the other Scotch streams; also in some of the Welsh rivers, from whence I have received fine specimens; in Ireland, near Enniskillen, and in the river Bann, which is noted for its fine pearls. They wade for them in the shallow pools, or take them by thrusting a long stick between the valves when the shell is open. When a number have been collected they are left to decompose, when the pearls drop out.† They may also be found in Kerry, in Donegal, in the Moy near Foxford, and in many of the other Irish rivers; and Mr. Buckland states, in the *Field*, December 10th, 1864, that they abound near Oughterard, and that a man called 'Jemmy the Pearl-catcher' told him he knew when a mussel had a pearl in it, without requiring to open it first, because 'she (the mussel) sits upright with her mouth in the mud, and her back is crooked', - that is, corrugated like a cow's horn. Bruce, in his *Travels* (1790), observes that the pearl-fishers of Bahrein, informed him that they had no expectation of finding a pearl when the shell was smooth and perfect, but were sure to find some when the shell was distorted and deformed; and he adds that this applies equally to the Scotch mussels. In France they also collect pearls from the pearl-mussels, and they generally sell them as *foreign* pearls. At Omagh, in the north of Ireland, there was formerly a pearl-fishery; and Gilbert, Bishop of Limerick, about 1094, sent a present of Irish pearls to Anselm, Archbishop of Canterbury. Scotch pearls were in demand abroad as early as the twelfth century. Suetonius says that the great motive of Caesar's coming to Britain was to obtain its pearls, and states

*The Times, December 24th, 1863.
†Tour in Ulster

that they were so large that he used to try the weight of them by his hand, and dedicated a breastplate made of them to Venus Genetrix.* According to Pliny, the island of Taprobane (Ceylon), was the most productive of pearls; and he considers that the most valuable were those found in the vicinity of Arabia, in the Persian gulf.

Lovell's comments on the Roman association with British pearls were echoed by Lionel Adams in his *The Collector's Manual of British Land and Freshwater Shells* (1884) thus:

Unio margaritifera (pearl-bearing)

This interesting species is to be found in rivers in mountain districts in several parts of Great Britain, and also in Ireland and Man. The pearls for which this shell was once eagerly gathered in the Tay, the Irt, and the Conway, are small and worthless compared with those of the East.

Suetonius says that Caesar was particularly attracted to Britain by the reports of pearls found there, and Pliny states that he covered a buckler with them, which he dedicated to Venus Genetrix.

Forbes and Hanley think that 'Caesar's buckler was more probably covered with the pearls from **Mytilus edulis'** (the common sea mussel). This, however, is not likely, as the pearls from this shell are exceedingly few and poor. Tacitus writes that they were of marine origin.

Pennant states that as many as sixteen pearls have been found in a single **Unio,** and he gives an account of pearls of value having been found in Donegal and the Conway.

The ancient writers agree in disparaging the British pearls, justly considering those from the East finer in size and quality.

* Camden's Britannia, p.962.

Tacitus mentions a theory current in his time that the dull reddish colour of our pearls was due to their being collected from cast-up shells instead of being gathered from living shells from the bottom of the sea; but he adds, with characteristic dry humour, that the fault probably lay in the pearls themselves, as otherwise his avaricious countrymen would have been sure to discover the best method of obtaining them.

Edwin Streeter, in his *Pearls and Pearling life*, (1886), records, under 'Scotch Pearls':

In the River Earn, a tributary of the Tay, and in the River Doon, pearl mussel gathering found among certain families not only a trade, but their sole means of livelihood. A more agreeable pursuit of the manual order can scarcely be imagined, and is, in point of fact, as pleasant as trout fishing on a hot day, and infinitely more profitable in the worst of times. Elaborate apparatus is not needed, all the skill necessary may be acquired in an hour, and experience avails little where there are no rules, and scarcely any dogma, to guide the manipulator. During the years 1761 to 1764, Pearls to the value of £10,000 were sent to London from the rivers Tay and Isla.

The revenue from this industry shortly afterwards began to decline, and the fishing was almost abandoned until the year 1860, when it was revived by a German, who prosecuted the almost forgotten trade for a while with such success that in 1865, the value of the pearls found was computed at £12,000 for that year alone - an assertion, however, that requires confirmation.

We believe that at the present time [1886], very little is done in the way of fishing for pearl-mussels in any of the rivers of Scotland, and that the search which is occasionally made by fishermen in the most favourable localities rarely proves remunerative. The industry has been rather discouraged, in consequence of its reputed interference with ordinary fishing.

Edward Step, writing about this species in his *Shell Life an Introduction to the British Mollusca (1901)* states:

... The Pearl Mussel is **U. margaritifer**, which has a shell of more oblong shape, much flattened, though of solid material. There is no gloss upon its rough, blackish-brown surface. Its length is about five and a half inches. The interior is pearly, but in this case the tint is flesh - colour, varied with stains of dull green. The animal is usually greyish with a tinge of red. It is a northern species, not occurring south of Pembrokeshire and Yorkshire. This is the species which produces the British pearls, at one time a somewhat important article of jewellery. The so-called "fishery" appears to have been abandoned, probably on the ground that "the game was not worth the candle." We are told that in the middle of the eighteenth century the Perth-shire Tay in three years contributed to London pearls valued at £10,000. These varied in hue from white, through pink and green to brown and black, the white predominating, and the pink most in demand. The peasants used to collect the mussels from the mountain streams just before the corn-harvest, and in the oldest and most deformed specimens they were most likely to find the pearls. Yet it is said that not one per cent of the shells contained a pearl, and that only one pearl in a hundred had any great value. The best of these, very regular in form, clear in colour, and the size of a pea, would be worth £3 or £4.

Richard Rimmer, in his *Shells of the British Isles, Land and Freshwater* (1907), referring to this species, mentiones the variety **sinuata** Lamarck from near Dumfries:

Var. l. **sinuata**. - Shell broader than the typical form, yellowish-brown; lower margin concave in the middle.

It occurs in some of the streams in the west of Scotland. I have met with it in the river Clouden, near Dumfries.

This reference is of considerable importance since it may represent the only authentic record of the live occurrence of the related species **Margaritifera auricularia** (Spengler) in Britain. This species differs from the pearl mussel **Margaritifera margaritifera** (Linnaeus) by the possession of lateral teeth , while the host fish for its parasitic glochidial stage is believed to be the Sturgeon, **Acipenser sturio**, a species which still occurs as a rare vagrant to the Clyde estuary. **Margaritifera auricularia** is now on the verge of extinction, being restricted to Spain. It formerly occurred in Britain and occurs as a fossil in the Thames Basin. Liverpool Museum, however, possesses a live caught shell in the J. W. Jackson collection which was reputedly collected from the River Clouden in 1865 by J. R. Hardy. It passed from him to W. Peace, then to Robert Standen in 1891 and from him to J. W. Jackson. J. W. Taylor wrote to Rimmer's daughter in 1917 inquiring about the locality, etc and received the following reply:

The **U. sinuatus** is common in the River Clouden, the bed of which is rocky and gravelly and the current runs very quickly, it flows through the grounds of Dalwoodie.

So far, recent visits to this area in 1991-2 have failed to reveal a single mussel so that the question as to whether the record is genuine or indeed if **Margaritifera** still exists at this site is unresolved.

Significantly this Clouden specimen was referred to in an article in the *Manchester City News* in January, 1894, in a report on a meeting of the Leeds and Manchester Conchological Society:

Unio sinuatus Lamarck. Many dredged from the Thames at Mortlake below Kew Bridge, (sent by Roy Dawkins), with bones and human skulls, from t heir fresh state they can scarcely be 'fossils', and probably may yet be discovered in the upper part of that river. It is a remarkable form, the only other localities where similar var. has been met with is in a river in Co. Waterford and the River Clouden, Dumfries.

W. J. Dakin in his book *Pearls*, published in 1913, writes:

...We shall conclude by a reference to the fresh-water pearl fisheries which are of importance, in the rivers of Europe and America.

The fresh-water pearl mussel of Europe is **Margaritana margaritifera.** It has been fished in Great Britain from the time of the Romans, and in the middle of the 18th. century large quantities of pearls were obtained from these shellfish in the river Tay.

The Scotch pearl fishery was stimulated again in 1860. The Irish fishery seems to have died out - the shellfish being much less common now than formerly. In 1906 the value of the pearls collected from the shellfish in the British Islands was put down as £3,000. No elaborate system of boats and dredges is used and probably all the shellfish are obtained by wading and feeling for the individual specimens.

On the continent the fishing has been carried on for a long time in the rivers of Finland. The pearls find their way chiefly into Russia. The fresh-water pearl mussel is also very common in the rivers of Germany and Bohemia. Quite recently the origin of pearls in these shellfish has been investigated in great detail by the Germans; reference will be made to their discoveries in a later chapter. The fishing has been very regular and carefully looked after in these countries. The rivers are inspected in springtime and the fishing takes place in summer. At the same time the recent pollution of water by factories has caused the usual decrease in the number of mussels. Pearls have also been obtained from the French rivers and in fact from many others in Europe which lack of space prevents us from mentioning.

The total value of pearls obtained on the continent of Europe in 1906 was about £20,000.

In America the fishery for fresh-water pearls is of greater importance, the value of pearls and shell together for 1906 being about £200,000.

The local historian and writer Donald Brown MacCulloch records their presence in his *Romantic Lochaber* of 1939 thus:

> Up in Glen Laragain (usually called 'the Glen' by Corpach inhabitants), which Prince Charlie traversed, there is a sedgy lochan, fringed with water lilies during summer, from which the Sheangain Burn flows east-wards. Among the long green goose-grass of the loch and burn fresh -water mussels are occasionally found, some of which contain pearls, but diligent search is necessary for any hope of success.

Sadly, this area has undergone considerable changes in land use during the intervening two hundred and fifty years which have elapsed since Bonnie Prince Charlie's visit. Few locals are even aware of the Loch's existence. In the 1970's this area underwent tree planting of Sitka Spruce, this process being accompanied by the construction of drainage ditches, etc., which resulted in the Loch being considerably reduced in volume. In fact it is now normally demarcated as a dried up depression subject to flooding during severe wet weather and presents a far different aspect from the one which existed during Bonnie Prince Charlie's time, and the continuing presence of pearl mussels might seem impossible. Such is not the case, however, for during the summer of 1993 a local historian braved the obstacles presented by the dense conifers and clambered upwards along the river banks to the loch above. Extensive searching brought a just reward with the discovery of a few live individuals nestling amongst the gravel. The pearl mussels concerned were about four and a half inches in length, which suggests that they are probably in the region of forty years or more in age, but at the same time indicates that they have been able to withstand the forestation modification to their environment so far. The future viability and survival of this historic location and its resident mussel population will depend upon whether juvenile mussels are able to survive and develop to adulthood, coupled with the future threat of further additional environmental pressures, inevitable during and after the felling of this commercial forest.

Further consideration is given to these problems later in the chapter on conservation and legislation.

PEARL FISHER CAMEOS

Martin Brooks

Martin Brooks of Scone, a Perth fireman, has seen a considerable decline in stocks during the past seventeen years or so of his passion for (part-time) pearl fishing. As he explains:

> I've seen the fishing on the Tay deteriorate over the years. There is far too much over-fishing and many of the beds are being killed off. We go out three or four times a week all over Scotland but it's getting harder to find good shells. I still find the occasional large pearl, but they are becoming harder to find. To get the big ones I have to fish the deep waters and that involves using sub-aqua equipment in the summer months when the water is not so cold.

Significantly, Martin mentions having to use sub-aqua gear to obtain decent sized pearls due to the mussels which contain them being relatively safe form the casual "amateur" who cannot reach them in the deeper pools. As a result the mussel has survived unmolested for a number of years and granted grace to lay down several annual layers of pearl material, resulting in a bigger pearl. Occasionally such pearl mussels become dislodged in periods of spate and are washed into shallower water, thus becoming available to the traditional pearl fisher. **The use of sub-aqua diving for pearl fishing,** please note, **has since been outlawed under the recommendations of the Bern Committee** , (detailed later in this book), in an attempt to safeguard the deeper lying populations of **Margaritifera.**

Martin continues by outlining his anger at pearl fishers who kill mussels in order to search for pearls. He declares:

I would like to see legislation that would make it illegal to kill, injure or destroy mussels. You do not have to kill the mussels. Pearls can be extracted without damaging the shellfish, but hardly any of the amateurs who are indiscriminately killing young mussels bother to replace them alive.

It is quite common to come across great piles of shells on the riverbank.

They kill the mussels by using a knife to open them and once the hinge is cut the mussel dies.

We use opening tongs to look inside. If there's a pearl you can get it out without damaging a mussel before putting it back in the river.

We have to put a stop to these people and we must act quickly to retain the mussel beds that are left.

Martin still fishes to this day, and was extremely active in drawing up the drafts for submission to, and lobbying of, the British authorities in regard to modification to the Wildlife and Countryside Act, making it illegal to kill or injure mussels.

Cairncross

Cairncross, the Perth Jewellers, have been commissioned to supply Scottish pearl set jewellery to a number of prominent people. Their publicity forward reads:

Cairncross is the home of Scottish river pearls.

Ours is a unique collection of unrivalled beauty and originality, fished from the fresh waters of the rivers Spey, Connan, Esk and Tay as they have been for generations.

Meticulously selected for their subtle hues of cream, white, peach and lilac, each pearl has a setting individually designed around it to enhance its natural beauty and bloom.

The drilling and setting of pearls is an increasingly rare skill which has been passed down through the generations.

Over the years, we have gained a unique understanding and love of pearls which is captured for eternity in the outstanding beauty of each piece of Cairncross Scottish river pearl jewellery.

These claims are well deserved, the firm being the major dealer in Scottish freshwater pearls, which are priced and graded here, being purchased direct from the pearl fishers. These pearls are then selected to decorate exquisite brooches with designs based on Scottish vegetation such as wild blaeberry, rowan, snowdrops, ferns, etc.; tie pins, some in the shape of golf clubs; earrings which again reflect vegetation such as Asphodel, orchids, Rowan sprigs, and so on; rings, pendants and last, but not least, necklaces. All of the designs are produced in-house, but the gold blanks are struck in Birmingham to Cairncross designs. The selection and grading of individual pearls for necklaces together with drilling are also carried out here and it is hardly surprising that Cairncross creations, featuring genuine Scottish-taken river pearls, are so popular regardless of price.

The late Alastair Cairncross, when asked to comment on Scottish pearls and the pearl mussel, remarked:

It is a houseproud creature which creates its own home by secreting fluids which crystallise to form conchiolin, the horny outside surface.

This is lined with a nacreous layer giving a lovely play of colour diffraction, breaking up white light into prismatic colours known as orient.

The mussel has a sensitive skin and when any irritant lodges in the shell it begins coating it with the same secretions which make up the shell.

The resulting pearl has a shape dependent on the position within the shell where the irritant lodged. The perfect ones are found within the flesh, or the loose flaps of skin on which the cells are found. Fine shapes are very scarce so it is difficult to make up good matches.

The beauty of the pearl lies in its fineness of orient, its quality of lustre and body colour. This depends on many factors - where the mussel has been living, chemicals in the water, and feeding matter.

Colours vary considerably from white through greys to gold and lilac. When compared with oriental pearls, the Scots pearl is like a plum still on the tree with the bloom on it, while the former are plums picked from the tree, polished and put in a shop window.

There is a lovely untouched quality about them which is highly distinctive, so that they are obviously real and cannot be mistaken for anything other than what they are.

Martin Young, general manager at Cairncross, is understandably greatly concerned at the continuing decline in the quantity and quality of the pearls which have been brought into Cairncross in recent years and says:

The mussels that are in the rivers are not producing pearls in the numbers and quality of past years. This is supported by reports from some of the more reliable pearl fishermen. The cause is put down to killing the mussel when opened, overfishing, and, we believe, pollution in the waters.

It would be a terrible disappointment if the pearls were to vanish from the rivers so maybe some kind of control over the fishing for them should be brought in - a licensing system may be the answer.

Pearl fishing is part of Scotland's heritage and so all feasible steps should be taken to protect the mussel.

Mr John Lochtie, Manager and Pearl Buyer at Cairncross commenting on recent legislation to protect the pearl mussel under the Wildlife and countryside Act is of the opinion that this legislation which has a maximum penalty of £2,000 for each breach, would deter the fair weather pearl fishers who kill all the mussels they examine. He continues:

I believe there are methods which can be used to extract pearls from the freshwater mussels that do not kill the molluscs. Also a reduction in the number of people fishing in the Scottish rivers which contain the mussels must be beneficial to its population spread. I feel the legislation may be difficult to enforce. However, it will hopefully frighten off a lot of people and leave the fishing to the more professional fishers.

Each year amateur pearl fishers bring in sizeable numbers of seed pearls which are virtually worthless, which if left to mature would otherwise have grown in size and have been much more useful and desirable and so this aspect makes us very aware of the importance of conservation.

Peter Goodwin

Peter James Goodwin was born in Liverpool in 1947, but left there in 1959 when his family moved to Camberly, Surrey, where he finished his formal education. In his book *The River and the Road, Journal of a Freshwater Pearl-Fisher* Peter describes this early part of his life, including his conversion to pearl fishing through the chance viewing of a television programme on Bill Abernethy in the autumn of 1970. We include the following extracts with his permission:

I went through the motions of swimming with the stream: school, work, college, university, dropping out, then work again. All the time an undercurrent of subversive influences pulled me into as yet uncharted waters. Contrary to his intentions, my father was responsible for this. Somehow, while trying to persuade me to accept a 'leg up' in the world through his contacts in the aircraft and oil industries, he managed instead to instil in me his own estranged love of country life. However, six weeks working for a greedy farmer in North Wales, in winter, knocked that out of me too, and I came back to a comfortable job near home.

It would have been comfortable but for night classes. Going to catch a bus to them was like the walk to the condemned cell. I slumped in the seat, staring in blank misery at the rain-streaked windows, hoping to miss the stop in the dark and that the bus would go on into the night forever.

Dropping out of university at twenty-two, I reckoned I was too old to run home with my tail between my legs. Part of the university course was a field trials job at Chipping Ongar in Essex. I took it to fill the void.

My first sight of the Essex countryside had been in February, when I was interviewed. My impression was of low hills in their umber tones of wet, ploughed earth, and elm copses drawn in charcoal against a grey sky. Even in April the brightest colour among the opening buds on the copses was the incongruous Tube, writhing like a red rattlesnake through the fields. For some reason it went all the way to Ongar.

Despite a fondness for hills much higher than those found in East Anglia, I looked forward to my stay. The field trials work was outdoors and meant plenty of travel. I found lodgings in High Ongar. In May the path to the tiny footbridge spanning the River Roding was heavy with the scent of hawthorn blossom in the overgrown hedgerows. Here, for the first time, I discovered some measure of contentment.

Despite good company, travel and work, I was marking time. Part of my life seemed destined to remain dormant. Somewhere, just out of reach, I knew there was a ready-made life that would fit me to perfection. Instead of reading about what other people were doing, I would either have something worth telling or be too taken up with my own affairs to bother.

One night, after walking my landlady's dog by the river, I was reading in front of the television. A programme called *Rivers of Pearl* caught my interest, and I laid my book aside for a while.

The film concerned a man called Bill Abernethy. He made a living fishing for freshwater pearls in the rivers of Scotland and claimed to be the only full-time, professional pearl-fisher in Britain, having that occupation marked in his passport.

In a state of mounting excitement, I devoured every word, trying to find out how, and where, the pearls were found. He was shown selling two or three weeks' pearls to a Perth jeweller for over £200, but though he'd made more in three weeks than I got in three months, I paid little attention to financial matters. What struck me was this man's living depended on nobody else. He took, at his leisure, what was there for the taking, submitting only to the dictates of weather and season. He went wherever the search for pearls took him, to places most of us enter only as tourists, searching in vain for roots that probably bind us to suburbia.

Torn from the limp complacency to which I was becoming accustomed, I was flung into a state of precarious indecision....

I didn't take long to come to a decision, even though decisiveness was out of character. ...I told my employers right away, but decided to stay till early spring if they didn't mind. It was too late in the year to go off half-cocked looking for something I knew nothing about. I had the winter and spring to find out all I could about the pearl mussel and pearl-fishing.

With such brief instruction in the pearl fishers' art it is hardly surprising that Peter's own early experiences proved far from successful, but fortune befell him through a chance meeting with Neil McCormack and his brother-in-law, Donald McGregor. Considerably impressed by their new found friend's enthusiasm they assisted in teaching him the secrets of their craft, which he still undertakes to the present day. Now, however, pearl mussels are less plentiful due to overfishing and Peter has played an active part in campaigning for their protection. His experiences as a pearl fisher form the basis for his book and provide an interesting insight to the pearl fishers life. He finishes his book by expressing the sentiments not only of himself, but also his fellows:

We feel no shame for the hedonistic approach we had to our profession but have been forced to recognise that we are an anachronism, a tribe of twentieth-century nomads who reaped a harvest they had not sown. My feelings, and probably those of my friends, when we set off for a river, were the same pangs of exhilaration and anticipation that gnawed at my innards as I lay in bed as a child, desperately awaiting the dawn of Christmas Day. To have had the same feeling 'going to work' defied the grim reality of a thousand Monday mornings.

Even near the close of a fruitless day's fishing, when the last glimmer of hope has been doused by a frozen, rain-sodden weariness, a couple of nice pearls from the last bag of shells can send you down the road in a state of exultation. To have found peace and deep contentment beyond the extremes of physical hardship, exhilaration and despair we endured is not the paradox it seems. Prospectors, mountaineers and

athletes reach these goals by the same route. Pearl
-fishers had the proud independence common to those
who share hardship or danger. I never imagined I'd
share such unselfconscious kinship, and now I fear its
coming loss.

Sadly, Peter's predictions concerning the
survival of this ancient craft seem well founded. All is
not yet lost, however, since it is possible that the
recent legislation coupled with public awareness may
result in a halt in the decline of Scottish mussel
stocks. Then, as rivers become cleaner and return to
their original unpolluted condition it is hoped that
recolonisation may take place. The considerable
studies which have been carried out on mussel
populations in recent years owe much to the co-
operation of two other pearl fishers, namely:

Neil and Mary McCormack

This husband and wife team have
championed the cause for protecting the pearl mussel
for about thirty years. Mary originates from a
traditional pearl fishing family, whilst Neil developed
the bug from them. In the early days of the fifties
pearl fishing provided a fair income, interspersed
with raspberry picking and other odd jobs as finances
required. As time passed, however, they recognised
the warning signs of declining populations through
overfishing, coupled with increasing pollution. In
response they contacted the Earl of Cranbrook,
drawing his attention to the problem, thus sowing the
first seeds for establishing legislation to protect this
species. In addition they were also instrumental in the
establishment of the research projects at Aberdeen
University, under the supervision of Dr. Mark Young,
on Scottish populations of the pearl mussel. This
co-operation continues and they have freely given

considerable time and support to the BRISC survey as well as assisting in providing information for, and contributing to, the drafting of proposals for European legislation. Their knowledge of the pearl mussel in the field is considerable and affords an untapped source for instructing others in the study of this species in the wild.

Snooks Peters

'Snooks' Peters was probably the last of the Ayrshire pearl fishers, and worked down the local coal mine. I first met him away back in the early sixties, at his council house at Patna, to enquire if he could obtain some examples of the pearl mussel for me to dissect. He readily agreed but was unwilling to disclose his source, suggesting that I should return the following week. This I did and was presented with half a dozen very large individuals, each over six inches in length. He assured me that he had obtained pearls from this population and showed me some which he kept in an aspirin bottle. Further interrogation failed to reveal their source, but local gossip claimed that he regularly fished the River Doon at crack of dawn in order to avoid the local gamekeepers.

Bill Abernethy

Like his father, Robert, and grandfather before him, William Stormont Abernethy, better known as 'Bill Abernethy', has practised the pearl fisher's art, being recognised as perhaps the last full time pearl fisher to work in Scotland. This is the more saddening when one considers the profession has been carried out for over two thousand years and that at the turn of the century there were over sixty full-time pearl fishers operating out of Perth alone.

Now nearly seventy, Bill, who once played professional football for Clyde and Arbroath, may still be seen as he carefully picks his way over the boulder-strewn river bed in search of mussels. This he achieves by peering through the tumbling water at the river bottom by means of his glass-bottomed jug which he had made specially for the task by an Ayrshire tin-smith. Suddenly, with a push of his stick, he lifts a large black shell from its watery den and quickly slips it into the canvas sack at his waist.

When asked why he still continues he replies:

There is an ancient Scottish law which gives the common man the right to fish for pearl mussels from July to August.

If I can get a living out of pearl fishing, I'm quite satisfied.

Although I fish all year round, I'll be lucky to make £4,000 this year. It's the pollution. The mussels just can't survive. Soon there will be no freshwater pearls.

Pearls come in every colour of the rainbow. It is just the colour and shape that gives them their value - really a matter of fashion. The brown ones are only worth a few coppers. They go to India where they are ground and sold as an aphrodisiac.

I've fished out pearls from Scottish rivers to provide jewellery for lots of Royal ladies, including the Queen and the Queen Mother. The Queen herself wears a brooch with pearls fished from the Spey which was presented to her after the opening of the Queen's Bridge, in Perth.

It's not really an easy way to earn a living. In fact it's downright hard sometimes when the weather is bad, but I wouldn't change it for worlds. I enjoy the fresh air and the solitude and some of the people I meet, and of course, the lure of another magnificent pearl.

I can't think of anything else I would rather do. Its
a fine, healthy job and you are your own boss. I can't see
me ever going down with stress. Can you?

Over the years Bill has witnessed the steady
decline of pearl mussel stock and has no illusions as
to the future:

Pollution is a problem. But these amateurs are
killing the mussel.

People who know anything about pearl fishing
don't destroy all the mussels to get pearls. With
experience it is possible to see which shells might
contain pearls and to remove them safely and return
the shell to the river. Most of the damage is being done
by people who think they can make a quick buck pearl
fishing on their holidays. Without experience to tell
whether a shell might have a pearl, they open and
kill hundreds of shells on Scottish rivers such as the
Tay and Spey.

Och, they're mostly just day trippers, people who
come up from Dundee for the week-end. They are just
amateurs; they try to open the mussels with a knife or
something, and if they can't they just break them open
with a stone. These amateur people are taking and
killing everything.

Bill's most famous discovery was that of
'Little Willie' also known as 'The Abernethy Pearl',
perhaps the most perfect Scottish specimen collected
in the last fifty years , which now occupies pride of
place in the shop of Cairncross, the Jewellers, at
Perth.   It was taken from the River Tay in 1967 and
has been highlighted through Bill's appearances on
television programmes such as *Jim'll fix it* and *What's
My Line?*. Bill describes its discovery thus:

The Abernethy Pearl, or 'Little Willie' as it's
known, was uncovered as I fished the River Tay. I was
knee-deep in a stretch with my father when I came

across this really odd-shaped mussel with a strange bubble-like protrusion on its shell. Pulling it open, I hoped to find a fair-sized pearl nestling inside but nothing prepared me for the size of this gem. It was sitting there in its shell, just like an egg. I jumped for joy in the river.

I had seen many beautiful pearls before and I have seen many since, but this was the most glorious of them all. I was speechless by its beauty. A freak of nature had produced a gem.

Returning to the shore Bill broke off a dock leaf and wrapped the pearl in it before hurrying to see Alastair Cairncross, the jeweller in Perth. The pearl was carefully examined and weighed and Bill continues:

Pearls are weighed in grains, with one grain equal to a carat, and most tend to weigh in around ten grains. But this beauty was a staggering forty-four grains and worth over ten thousand pounds even in those days. So far I haven't been able to part with it, despite offers that flood in from all over the world.

News of the size and value of Bill's find soon spread like wildfire throughout the surrounding area and Bill recalls:

The week after I found it, the banks of the Tay were lined with people using all sorts of strange methods to get rich quick. Of course their enthusiasm died off pretty quickly. But as you see I'm still very much at it. Every so often I find a bigger pearl than 'Little Willie', but it is usually out of shape or a poor colour. I won't tell you exactly where I found Little Willie, because there might be another one just like it hiding down there, and I wouldn't want anyone to beat me to it.

'Little Willie' graced Cairncross' shop for a period extending over twenty years. In fact it was there so long that no-one could remember, after Alastair Cairncross died, whether or not Bill had sold the pearl to Cairncross. The jewellers thought that he had done so. Bill thought he had not. Bill explains:

When I took the pearl to Cairncross I was paid a nominal sum, so Mr. Cairncross could keep the pearl on display as an attraction. Nothing was written down. In the jewellery business your word is as good as your bond.

Fortunately Mrs Flora Rennie who now owns Cairncross intervened, a settlement was made and Cairncross kept custody of the magnificent pearl "to promote the interests of pearls in Scotland". As Mrs. Rennie explains, Little Willie is the jewel in the crown of Scottish river pearls and its fame attracts many visitors to our shop each year. The opportunity to acquire it so that it would remain in Perth and indeed Scotland was not one to miss.

EUROPE

Frequent reference has been made to freshwater pearls from mainland Europe. In 1906 the total value of pearls obtained was reported as being in the region of some £20,000. In the past the industry was relatively extensive, thus Schroeter writing in 1779 on the Norwegian pearl fisheries, states:

The writers, especially Pontoppidan, believe that the pearls from the mussels of Norway are finer and better than those from other places. Especially famous are the ponds and streams of the west-coast. Pontoppidan appears to speak of river mussels in general, rather than the pearl mussel in particular.

He says that the most famous pearl-fishery, run under Royal authority, is in the Bishopric of Christianssand, where the majority of pearl-streams are. The pearls, which are fished for around mid-summer's day, belong to the Queen of Norway alone, and the fishery is controlled by an officer, appointed by the Queen. The pearls found here, are mainly white, and silvery, but according to jewellers, they have not the quality of oriental pearls. Some, however, have the size and beauty of an East-Indian pearl. In Sweden, pearl mussels have been found which are a quarter of an ell long, and as broad as a grown man's hand.

He continues, regarding Lapland:

The pearl mussels of Lapland and Voigtland are large and fine, and fit my description almost exactly. They are found in some rivers, apart from those in which the Lapps are permitted to fish. Their pearls, as Scheffer observes, are not to be looked down on. Olaus Magnus believes that the paleness of the pearls is due to the cold climate of their place of origin. Only Scheffer doubts this. One cannot deny that the majority lack the beauty which is praised on the oriental pearl. There are, however, some found which have a beauty and worth. When these are ripe, then they have a full spherical shape, but the majority are unripe and these have one half round, the other half flat. These are beautiful and shiny on the round side, and on the flat side they are yellow, or earth-coloured, brown and dark. Scheffer testifies that he had seen a pearl from Bothnia which was so large, so perfectly round, beautiful and of such vivid colour that a prominent lady wished to pay 120 Kaiserguilden for it. A jeweller attests, that were he to possess such a pearl, he would not part with it for less than 500 Kaiserguilden. The pearls, which are not ripe, are attached to the shell, whereas those which are ripe are free, and fall out when the shell is opened.

He describes those from the Voigtland thus:

The River Elster in the Voigtland has been known for a long time as a famous pearl-stream. Most of the older writers are of one voice, that this river yields the most beautiful pearls of all the European rivers, although Boodt believes that pearls from some of the Bohemian rivers are more beautiful. In Voigtland, the pearl mussel is known as the 'Perletroge'. Oelsnitz observes that pearls from this stream were of such a size and beauty, that the then King of Poland, August, ordered that only certain people could fish there. The present Queen of Poland, the Duchess of Zeitz, possesses a necklace made of such pearls. The catalogue of the Royal 'Naturalien Keimmer' in Dresden states - 'The pearls from the Elster are as beautiful in regards to size, roundness and shine, as the most beautiful oriental pearl'. I have already described the mussel itself, and in Tab. IV fig. 1, I illustrate a mussel from the Elster. In this, there is a pearl, directly under the exterior swelling. This large pearl is only half-grown, but doubtless could be made as beautiful as an oriental pearl, were it to be given to a fine artist. That the most of the pearls do not ripen, and do not possess the shine, or the usual fine lustre, I am hesitant to mention. Good, ripe pearls approach the oriental in beauty, but when examples of both are compared, the pearls from the Elster do not seem any better than those from inland rivers.

Referring to the pearl fisheries of Franconia he continues:

The pearl mussels from Franconia are described in the *'Frankische Sammlungen'*. I cannot use this, as I do not possess a copy of the book, and neither do any of my friends. To please the majority of my readers, I shall quote an extract from a letter from a friend in Erlangen. The fact that a pearl fishery was discovered in Franconia was due to a peasant who had found some pearls, and had exchanged them with a Jew for rings and other trivialities. Through this, the authorities heard of the find, and informed the ruling Prince. These mussels containing pearls are found in two places in the Oberland: - near Himmeltron, and near Rehav. This latter place is where the most beautiful pearls are found. The river at Himmeltron is the 'Weisser Main' [White Main], at Rehav it is simply known as the Perlenbach' [Pearl stream] - both these rivers are tributaries of the River Main. It has been known for approximately fifty years that these streams produce pearls. It is now very difficult to find a pearl mussel for foreign friends and 'Kabinetts' and even more difficult to obtain a good pearl, as all good pearls have to be surrendered to the ruling Prince. Some are quite excellent, and the late Margravine of Bayreuth made a selection, and had bracelets and necklaces made. These are now in the possession of the Duchess of Wurtenberg. Lesser mortals have to be satisfied with less good examples.

All pearl mussels from Franconia have been eaten by worms. I have the good fortune to possess three Rehav pearls of the highest quality. The first is brown, and when I filed a notch in it, I found it to be quite solid, and brown throughout. I can say with confidence that it is unripe, and that it would never at any time have possessed a better colour, as I believe that it must have been taken from a very old or sick mussel. This pearl is round like a ball. The second is elliptoid, and has been in the hands of an artist, as it has been worked, and a hole has been bored through. It has the most beautiful pearl-colours, which one expects to find on such a good example, except that there is a matt-white band around the middle, which would perhaps have disappeared, had the artist polished it further, and made it a little smaller. The third has a more beautiful lustre. It is the smallest of my collection, about the size of a sugar-pea. it would have great worth, had it not a brown, unripe part, where it must have been attached to the mussel. On some examples this does not hinder one from setting it in a jewel, and thus hiding the unripe part.

And briefly he outlines the 18th Century pearl fisheries which occurred in the Livonia area:

It is to be regretted that Herr Fischer, who has spoken about Livonia's natural rarities, and the local pearl mussels, does no more than repeat the opinion of Mylius and Jetze. His excuse is, that he did not have the opportunity to seek mussels and pearls for himself, or report on the fishing methods employed. I take from this that the pearl fisheries in Livonia must not be very productive. I will make the following remarks, taken from my sources, about the history of this pearl fishery. Mylius reports that an inspector of fisheries was appointed soon after the turn of the century. Jetze, however, in his book of 1749 says that pearls had only begun to have been fished for in the last three years. The first mentioned fishery must have died out. It follows that this fishery could not have been very productive, although Jetze states that Livonian pearls approach the oriental in shine and size.

Kelch says in his 'Livonian Chronicles' that pearls were found in the streams of Meetz. This report dates however, from the time of King Karl XI of Sweden. a Swede, Hedenberg, is quoted as saying that pearls are diligently sought for. This report dates from 1742, and Fischer states that the fishery went into decline after this.

Martini quotes from Mylius, that pearls can only be found in ponds and streams with fresh, clear water, in which trout and loaches are also found. Pearls are found between the middle of July and the middle of August. Fischer states that the 'Schwarzbach' in the 'Wenduscher Kreis' has the most famous pearl fishery. Pastor Hupel, in his Livonian Topography, p. 134 names this as a pearl-rich stream. Herr Hupel, my countryman, says further, that over forty streams and lakes yield pearls, but most are not worth the trouble to fish, with the exception of the 'Schwarzbach', where pearls the size of a pea may be found, but these are mostly unripe. Second only to the Schwarzbach, the R. Tirse is also a well-known pearl fishery. An old tavern in the parish of Tirse has for many years had the name 'Perlekroghs'.

In 1848 Schrenk, writing on the Mollusca of Livonia, states:

I have not so far had the opportunity to observe its occurrence, and therefore take the following notes of its localities from Fischer's Naturg. Livlands, 1791: It chooses for its abode preferably small rivers and becks with hard water, which specially contain loach and trout, where the mussels lie close to one another, deeply buried in deep pools filled with sand and rubbish. The Schwarzbach in the Oppenkalnschen Kirchspiele of the Walkschen district was famed for its pearl-mussels, and then furthermore the little river Tirse, where an old inn under the country-seat Druenen in the Tirsenschen Kirchspiele of the Walkschen district took the name Perlekroghs (pearl ale-house).

Hupel noted in his Topography of Livland, on there being well on to forty waters in Livland (the Ostsee provinzen?) where pearls had been fished. The pearl-fishery in Livland had the attention of two reigns in being cultivated and occupied for a long time: for already in 1694 the Swedish King Charles XI issued a mandate, through which the pearl-fishing on the crown lands in Livland, Estland, and Ingermanland was declared Royal, and an Inspector appointed over the same. As expectation had run too high and was deceived, the business consequently fell into decay. Under Russian authority however, in the reign of the Empress Elizabeth, it was taken up again upon the instigation of one named Hedenburg, and was carried on for some time with a great deal of energy and expense, whereby a great many beautiful pearls of the size of peas were obtained. The expenses however, outweighed the gains to such an extent that the whole business was again abandoned.

The species was also recorded by J. H. Kawall in 1869 in his Courland list in the *Bulletin des Seances de la Societe Malacologique de Belgique* thus:

Frequent in Livone, and said to be found also in Courland, in the Courbe, but I have not yet found it. I reserve for another paper, and account of Pearl-fishing in Livonie.

Pearls were also frequently fished in Russia, but due to their relative isolation form the rest of Europe following the formation of the Soviet Union in 1917, little information is available to us in the west regarding these fisheries. However, we may deduce that the industry must have been fairly extensive if the vast numbers of freshwater pearls incorporated in Russian religious icons, clerical cassocks, pearl jewellery and 18th and early 19th century portraits are anything to go by. Many of these were almost certainly of Russian origin, but in addition, the major portion of the pearls obtained throughout the rest of Europe together with Russia's neighbours in the Far East, were destined for Russia to satisfy the immense market there from the sixteenth up to the twentieth century.

Following the upsurge of the Industrial Revolution at the end of the eighteenth century, European mussel population decreased markedly so that they may now be considered as on the verge of extinction in the major part of their former range. The reasons for this were initially overfishing, followed by pollution of surface waters through industrial waste, and more recently the increased indiscriminate use of artificial organic compounds in the form of pesticides and fertilisers for agriculture.

JAPANESE PEARLS

Japan now occupies centre stage of the world's pearl trade, being responsible for the major portion of cultured marine pearl production using Mikimoto's techniques. The marine oysters used, **Pinctada furcata**, produce Akoya pearls, measuring from two to ten millimetres, which form the backbone of Japan's cultured pearl industry. However this has not always been so. Thus Kaempfer, in his *History of Japan* (1690), writes, under *Climate and Minerals of Japan* :-

Pearls, by the Japanese called Kainotamma, which is as much as to say, Shell Jewels, or Jewels taken out of Shells, are found almost every where about Saikokf in oysters and several other Sea-shells. Everybody is at liberty to fish them. Formerly the Natives had little or no value for them, till they were appris'd of it by the Chinese, who would pay good prices for them, the Chinese Women being very proud of wearing Necklaces, and other Ornaments of Pearls. The largest and finest Pearls are found in a small sort of oyster, call'd Akoja, which is not unlike the Persian Pearl-shell, much of the same shape, both valves shutting close , about a hand broad, exceeding thin and brittle, black, smooth and shiny on the outside, within pretty rough and unequal, of a whitish colour and glittering like Mother of Pearl. These Pearl-shells are found only in the Seas about Satzuma, and in the gulf of Omura. Some of the Pearls weigh from four to five Condonins, and these are sold for a hundred Colans apiece. The inhabitants of the Riuku Islands buy most of those which are found about Satzuma, they trading to that Province. Those on the contrary which are found in the Gulf of Omura, are sold chiefly to the Chinese and Tunquinese, and it is computed that they buy for about 3000 Thails a year. This great profit occasioned the strict orders, which were made not long ago by the Princes both of Satzuma and Omura, importing, that for the future there should be no more of these oysters sold in the market with other Oysters, as had been done formerly. I procured some in private from Omura, not without great difficulty. I was told a very extraordinary thing about this sort of pearls, and strongly assured of the truth of the fact, which is, that they have somewhat of a prolifick quality, by virtue of which, when some of the largest are put into a box full of a peculiar Japanese cheek varnish, made of another shell call'd Takaragai (which I shall describe in another place) one or two young pearls will grow on the sides, and when come to maturity, which they do in about three years' time, drop off. These Pearls, by reason of their scarcity, are kept in private Families, and the possessors seldom part with them, unless upon urgent necessity. All this however I deliver only upon hearsay, having myself seen none of this sort of Pearl. There is another Shell, which sometimes yields Pearls, found plentifully upon all the Japanese Coasts, and called by the Natives Awabi. It is an Univalve, in shape almost oval, pretty deep, open on one side, where it sticks to the Rocks and to the bottom of the Sea, with a row of holes, which grow bigger, the nearer they come to the circumference of the Shell, rough and limy on its outward surface, frequently with Corals, Sea-plants and other Shells sticking to it, on the inside an exquisite Mother-of -Pearl's glimmering, sometimes raised into whitish excrescencies, which are likewise observed in the common Persian Pearl-shell. A great lump of flesh fills the cavity of this Shell, for which sole reason they are looked for by Fishermen, being a very good commodity for the market. They have an Instrument made on purpose to pull them off from the sides of the Rocks, to which they stick close. Another Shell, the name of which I could not learn, yields a very large Pearl, which sometimes weighs from five to six Condonins, but they are of a dirty yellow colour, ill shap'd, and worth but little. A pretty good sort of Pearl, is sometimes observed to grow in the very Flesh of a Shell, which is called by the Natives Tairaggi, and is found in the Gulf of Arima, between Janagava and Isafaje. It is a flat sort of a Shell, oblong, almost triangular, a little crooked on each side, about a span and a half long, and a span broad, where broadest, thin, transparent, smooth, and polished like Horn, but very brittle.

He finishes this section on *The Fish and Shells of Japan* with a section on *Oysters and Shells* illustrated by figures 66-69:-

Oysters and Shells

All sorts of oysters, muscles and shells, of which there is a great plenty and surprising variety in the Japanese seas, are eat, none excepted, raw, pickl'd, salted, boil'd, or fryed. They are daily gathered on the Coasts in low water. Divers dive for them to a considerable depth. Others fish them with nets. The following sorts are the most common and best known.

Awabi

Awabi, which I have already mentioned, when I spoke of the pearls of this Country, is an open Univalve, as big as a middle sized Persian Pearl shell, but deeper. (Fig.66). They lie deep underwater, sticking fast to rocks, or to the bottom of the Sea, from whence they are taken up by Fishermen's wives, they being the best Divers of the Country. They go down arm'd with darts and long knifes, to defend themselves against Kayes and Popesses, and when they see an Awabi, they pull it off suddenly before the animal is aware, because otherwise it would fasten itself to the rocks, or to the bottom of the Sea, so strongly, that no force would be strong enough to tear it off. This shell is fill'd with a large piece of flesh of a yellowish, or

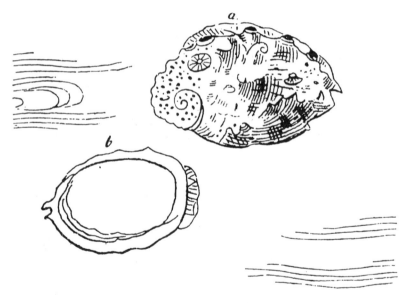

Awabi, an open Univalve

whitish colour, and a very tough substance, though without fibres. They say, it was the common food of their necessitous Ancestors, in memory whereof when they entertain company at dinner, they always provide a dish of it. It is also become a custom with them, as well among the vulgar, as among people of quality, that when they send one another presents of money, cloth, stuffs, fruits, or anything else, a string, or at least a small bit of the dried flesh of this shell is sent along with them, as a good Omen, and in order to put them in mind of the Indigency of their Forefathers. The flesh is cut into thin slices or strings, which are extended on a board, and dried. A large Pearl is found sometimes in this Shell, but of an ugly yellowish colour, a deformed shape and of no value.

The shell depicted belongs to the marine gastropod genus **Haliotis** commonly known as Abalones, Ormers or Sea Ears. They are vegetarians and distributed worldwide from low tide level to depths of several hundred feet. The flattened, ear-shaped shell has a series of holes on the body whorl through which water and waste products are passed. The pearly interior with its single, central muscle scar, is often used as a source of mother-of-pearl. The animal is often used as food, the larger species of California being farmed for this purpose. Abalone 'pearls' are irregular in shape and of the Baroque type.

Kaempfer continues with Mirakai, or freshwater mussel, which is the same species, **Margaritifera margaritifera** as that found in Scotland. He writes:

Mirakai

Mirakai is the common black freshwater Muscle, which is found also in our Rivers and Lakes in Germany.

Famaguri

Famaguri, (Fig 68), are bivalves much of the same shape and bigness, but thicker, smooth and white within, without of a brown or chestnut colour. Divers curious figures are painted on the inside, and they serve as an Amusement to the Court of the Dairi, or Ecclesiastical Hereditary Emperor, who play with them after the following manner. Large heaps are thrown on the ground, and every one of the Company having taken his Portion, he wins, that can shew the most pairs. Every pair hath proper hooks, by the means of which they are easily known, and brought together, tho' never so much mix'd. The best are gather'd, and in greatest plenty upon the coasts of Quano.

The exact identification of this species is uncertain, but includes the freshwater mussel **Hyriopsis schlegelli** which occurs in Lake Biwa and was originally used for production of blister pearls.

In the late 1920's the Japanese commenced cultivating freshwater pearls in Lake Biwa by implanting pieces of mantle tissue into the mantle of living mussels to produce non-nucleated pearls. Each animal may have anything from thirty up to a maximum of fifty implants, which take about three years to develop. In recent years Lake Biwa has become polluted by pesticides and agricultural fertilisers to such an extent that juvenile mussels no longer develop in the lake in sufficient numbers to support the industry. As a result, trials have been made to produce them in tanks in the laboratory, but the mussels so produced tend to be weak.

In 1971 one farmer, Syoichi Kitao, established a new farm in the cleaner waters of the Shintone River, with the innovation of inserting solid nuclei using Mikimoto's method for implanting into marine

Famaguri.

Famiguri, bivalves smooth and white within,
without of a brown or chestnut colour.

oysters, **Pinctada furcata**, at the same time. He obtains young mussels from the river and places them in holding baskets after having inserted solid mother-of-pearl nuclei produced from North American freshwater mussel shells. He refers to his venture in the National Geographic Magazine for August 1985 thus:

> I left Lake Biwa for clean water. In 1971 I came to this river and started the Daiko Pearl Company. Here I grow all the young mussels I need. Just look at the size and condition of these. The strong current carries plenty of food. My animals grow far bigger than they would lying in a still lake. See the thirty pearls here in the mantle. Now I'm going to show you something I've never shown anyone from the outside. You see, a spectacular round, pink pearl of some fourteen millimetres. I've married two cultures, freshwater mussel with South Sea oyster techniques. Instead of just traditional mantle-tissue nucleating with mussels, I'm inserting shell-bead nuclei inside their bodies, just as farmers do with saltwater oysters. I never use a nucleus more than nine millimetres, so that these pearls have thick nacre, not like the akoyas. Once I made seventeen millimeter. My ambition is to be first to culture a round twenty-millimeter freshwater pearl. When I get that, I will present it to the President of the United States, not the Emperor. Why? Because the U. S. is my best customer, and I'm going to say 'Thank you!'

UNITED STATES

Following on from the passage mentioned in our previous chapter on the historical aspects of Scottish pearl fishing, W. J. Dakin, in his 1913 book, *Pearls*, continues:

In America the fisher for fresh-water pearls is of greater importance, the value of pearls and shell together for 1906 being about £200,000. The fishery dates back to the time of the ancient inhabitants and remains of the shells are found in Indian mounds. The modern fishery was stimulated into growth in 1857 by the finding of a very fine pearl weighing 93 grains at Notch Brook near Paterson (New Jersey). It was sold to the Empress Eugenie for 12,500 francs.

The news of this discovery had an effect, similar on a small scale, to the discovery of gold. The American pearl mussels are found in rivers over a very wide area of the States and Canada. ...

W. Harrison Hutton in his 1917 paper to Leeds Conchological Club enlarges upon this and writes:

America is deservedly noted for its freshwater pearls. Columbus in his third voyage, 1494, when he entered the Gulf of Pana says the natives 'came to the ships in their canoes in countless numbers, many of them wearing pieces of gold on their breasts and some with bracelets of pearls on their arms, seeing which I was much delighted'. Of course he inquired where they found such treasures and they innocently informed him, directing him northward and westward behind the country they occupied.

The most recent pearl fisheries in the United States are those of the rivers and freshwater lakes, especially those in the Mississippi valley: they produce annually about a half-million dollars worth of pearls, many of which compare well with those of the oriental seas. The first realization of the value of American freshwater pearls occurred not much over fifty years ago in New Jersey, when a person named David Howell or Paterson, a shoemaker, who went out of an evening to the neighbouring streams to gather mussels, which he fried for his supper. On his return from one of his visits to Notch Brook, one of the streams, and the mussels were fried as usual, one of them was found to contain a round large pearl weighing nearly four-hundred grains, but spoiled with the heat and grease. If uninjured its value would possibly have exceeded $25,000. He instantly set about hunting for others, and his example was followed by several other neighbours. A few days after one named Jacob Quackenbush, a carpenter, found a fine pink pearl weighing ninety-three grains, which he sold for $1,500, to a Mr. Tiffany of Tiffany and Co., New York City. This pearl was sold in Paris for Tiffany's to a French dealer for 12,500 francs and the dealer to the Empress Eugenie (its present owner), and its present value will be about or over $10,000. In 1857 $25,000 worth of pearls were collected from these waters and came into New York market, the present value of which would be $200,000. In 1878 $25,000 worth were collected in the district of Waynesville in Little Manne River, Ohio. In 1901 to 1906 a fairly good number of pearls were found in American rivers (Freshwater) varying in value from $30, $60, $600 to $800 each, besides millions of dollars worth of smaller gems. Besides the collection of pearls from the American rivers there is the collection of pearl shells of which about 35,000 tons are collected annually in the Mississippi valley (1901 - 1910), the value of which varies from $29 to $50 per ton. These shells are used in the manufacture of buttons, fancy buckles, mother-of-pearl goods and other ornaments and ornamental work.

Sadly, with the usual objective of financial gain far outstripping any consideration for the sustainability of native freshwater mussel stocks, the Americans overfished their rivers for the pearly freshwater mussel shells to such an extent that the populations declined to virtual extinction in many areas. This decline was principally due to uplifting every mussel encountered, regardless of size, with the result that populations were unable to breed sufficiently to maintain stability. In response, the United States Government commissioned numerous surveys and studies on the group, in an attempt to rectify the problem.

As far back as the 1880's, scientists were warning of the dangers and attempting to find substitutes. In a paper in the *American Naturalist* for June 1883, the American, William Dall, refers to one such attempt to create metallic pearl buttons based on the physical structure of mother-of-pearl thus:

The shells consist of two parts, the epidermis and the shelly matter proper; the latter is usually composed of more or less different layers. The epidermis is of a horny texture and chiefly composed of a substance called conchioline. It is usually colored darker or lighter brown, and may be entirely dissolved in caustic alkali, but is not affected by ordinary acids, and serves as protection for the carbonate of lime of which the true shell is composed. This carbonate of lime may be deposited in prisms, as of arragonite, in amorphous or fibrous layers, or as 'mother-of-pearl'. In all cases it contains more or less animal matter which binds it more firmly together. The pearly lustre is caused by the action upon light of the minute layers of which the nacre is composed. These layers are microscopically corrugated, and their edges meet the rays of light and decompose them partly like drops in a rainbow, producing the play of varied colours. This has been proved in two ways, first by digesting mother-of-pearl in acid till all the lime is dissolved. A pellucid membrane, representing the animal matter still remains, and if undisturbed still shows the iridescence. But if pressed flat so as to remove the corrugations, it also loses its pearliness. Again, by means of a diamond splinter and an engine invented by Mr. Barton of the British Mint, similar corrugations have been engraved on the polished surface of a steel button with the result of producing the pearly play of colours, a process which would have been commercially valuable could the engraved buttons have been kept from tarnishing. There are also fine superficial lines on pearly surfaces which may add to the effect. These run in various directions, are 1/7700 of an inch apart according to Dr. Carpenter and may be due to minute cilia with which the mantle is provided.

Pearl buttons were also manufactured in Europe, the Russians having a fairly extensive industry between the wars, utilizing the shells of **Unio**, those of the pearl mussel, **Margaritifera** not normally being used due to the shell readily flaking. In Britain, Birmingham was a leading centre not only for buttons but also, in the middle of the Nineteenth century, for the production of mother-of-pearl inlay work to decorate paper-mache trays, tables, chairs and other trinkets. The mother-of-pearl used originated from the vast quantities of freshwater mussel shells imported from the United States. There is a local tradition that Birmingham town hall is built upon foundations composed of the discarded shell remains from this industry.

In the United States overfishing was partly resolved in the 1940's with the innovation of plastic buttons. Regardless of this welcome reduction, excessive overfishing continues to this day in order to provide nuclei for the Japanese cultured pearl industry. This factor, coupled with the continued development of hydroelectric schemes, road developments, channellization, and agricultural run-off, has caused a continued decline, with around fifty species now being considered totally extinct.

Raymond Neck, writing in 1982 on the freshwater mussels of Texas, provides the following information:

Freshwater clam shells or products made from shells have been widely utilized in an ornamental manner during historical times. Primary utilization of shell material by Americans was as buttons. Thousands of pounds of shell were removed from American rivers during the latter half of the nineteenth century and the first half of the twentieth century. Indeed, essentially all of our early studies on ecology, growth and zoogeography of freshwater clams resulted from commercially orientated studies by the U.S. Bureau of Fisheries. Utilization of buttons made from mother-of-pearl of freshwater mussels in Texas was concentrated on several species with strong thick shells in each area. The only species utilized in the valley was **Cyrtonaias tampicoensis.**

In kind with their marine relation, freshwater clams also produce pearls in response to irritants. A thriving pearl industry developed around Caddo Lake in the early twentieth century. An estimated $100,000 worth of pearls was removed from Caddo Lake in 1912, a year considered poor in comparison with previous years. Interestingly, the shell resource of the Caddo Lake area was not utilized by the button industry because of transportation costs and competitive high local wages ($3 per day in oil fields). Fine white pearls were obtained from **Megalonaias gigantea** and **Tritigonia verrucosa** while colored pearls were found in **Plectomerusdombeyanus;** pearl color is the same as the nacre color for a particular individual.

Freshwater pearls are of minor significance in our modern economy, but are occasionally publicized. However, there is one stream in Texas which still produces significant amounts of pearls. Individuals of **Cyrtonaias tampicoensis** in the Concho River in the vicinity of San Angelo, Tom Green Co., produce high-quality pearls of a purplish color. A local jeweller purchases 500 to 1200 of these pearls each summer on an *ad libitum* basis from local residents, primarily adolescents. Most pearls vary from 3 to 8 mm in diameter; the largest known is 13 mm in diameter. While freshwater clams no longer provide large amounts of pearls, these animals are still a part of the modern pearl industry. Thousands of pounds of freshwater clam shells are annually exported to Japan for use in the cultured pearl industry. Pearl culture began in 1912 when Kokichi Mikimoto developed successful methods in Japan. Various potential nuclei, i.e. irritants, were tested. The best nuclei were those made from freshwater clam shells. Primary locations of diverse, high-density populations of freshwater clams in the world are eastern North America (especially the Mississippi River system) and mainland China. For some years China has had essentially no trade with Japan because of political factors; therefore, the Japanese cultured pearl industry has depended entirely upon shell from the United States.

Fuller listed the major impacts of collecting for the cultured pearl industry in 1974 as follows:

1. reduction of brood stock to a level that reproduction may not equal mortality;
2. physical alteration of substrate of mussel bed areas;
3. stress-induced abortion of brooded young following disturbance at improper times for successful reproduction;
4. 'waste deaths' of juveniles below legal and/or utilitarian limits; and
5. uprooting of adults which are often not able to rebury themselves correctly.

Fuller considers the use of diving gear to be the 'greatest threat to commercially valuable mussels today'.

The total tonnage of clam shell removed from the waters of Texas is unknown, although the figures must be large. Reports of shell removed from various reservoirs in Texas by a single company give a total of 3,820,252 pounds during 1978 -1981. Shell operations by other companies are occurring in other drainages and reservoirs. Preferred species in Texas are **Amblema plicata, Quadrula apiculata** and **Proptera purpurata**. During the drought of 1978 many Texas reservoirs were at record low levels, allowing easy access to numerous clams by 'amateur' shell collectors who sold their booty to shell companies for 20 cents per pound. Enterprising persons hired several children to dive and collect clam shells. One such person accumulated over 1100 pounds on his most successful day of operation. The shell industry in Texas has reached the economic point such that one company is considering some form of clam cultivation in order to increase and ensure a quantity of shell for their customers. Such methods have been successful elsewhere (Jones 1940).

Although the lag time between shell collection and purchase report by the shell company is unknown, certain patterns of harvesting are evident. Most harvesting occurs during the warm season. Harvesting peaks are evident in drought years (1970 and 1980) with much less activity in wet years when the reservoirs are full (1979) or flooding (1981). Harvesting activities have been concentrated in Eagle Mountain Lake (Tarrant Co,) and Lake Lewisville (Denton Co,) in the Trinity River drainage. Minor amounts have been removed from Lake Brownwood (Brown Co,) and Cedar Creek Reservoir (Henderson and Kaufman Counties).

To prepare a nucleus for a cultured pearl, the thickest part of the clam shell is cut into strips and then cubes which are then ground and polished into a spherical shape. These pellets are then sold to pearl farmers who insert the pellet into an incision in the foot of three-year old Japanese pearl oysters. The oysters are then place in submerged wire cages for an average of three years. Pearls are then removed, graded, sorted and polished.

Freshwater clams are also utilized to a minor extent in art crafts. Some of the larger shell shops in coastal Texas sell freshwater clam shells as well as the more colorful and more popular marine mollusc shells. Some of the naiad shells found in shops in south Texas are imported from Mexico. Shell waste from the cultured pearl industry can be manufactured into craft products.

Since 1982 there has been considerable progress to protect and conserve the United States freshwater mussel populations through State and National Legislation. Also, intensive studies have been undertaken on propagating individual threatened species, with the intention of future re-introduction.

In the early 1980's the Camden, Tennessee firm of John Latendresse and his Japanese wife, Chessy, supplied mussel shells from the Mississippi River Basin to Japan for nuclei production, as well as designing and selling pearl jewellery using natural American freshwater pearls. Over the years they had noted a marked decline in both quality and numbers of natural American freshwater pearls and decided to farm nucleated pearls direct. Several of these farms, which consist of nucleated native freshwater mussels suspended in plastic tubes, were set up at suitable sites in the Mississippi and Tennessee River Valleys. The nucleation process was initially carried out by Chessy, who had been taught how to insert pearl nuclei into oysters in her native Japan, and subsequently by employees trained by her. The resultant nucleated pearls are of high quality but, obviously, natural American freshwater pearls still have a greater value. An advantage of growing them direct is that by using different species characterised by distinct nacre colours, it is possible to produce nucleated pearls of similar colours such as pink, yellow, white, and so on. In 1990 Amie Brautigan, Deputy Chairman of the International Union for Conservation of Nature/Species Survival Commission's Trade Specialist Group wrote:

One of the most heavily represented groups of animals listed as threatened or endangered under the United States Endangered Species Act is the family Unionidae, the naiads, a highly diverse group of freshwater bivalves, most of which are endemic to the United States. Of the 297 taxa native to North America thirteen are believed to be extinct; thirty-five are listed as endangered, and a further fifty-five are or have been candidates for listing under the Act. Review of status information for the remaining two-thirds of the taxa in this group and state endangered and threatened species lists would be likely to add a considerable number of taxa to what should be considered an 'absolute minimum' list of threatened species.

While over-exploitation of naiads and the freshwater pearl oysters of the genus **Margaritifera** for the pearl button and pearl industry reduced populations of these animals in the United States at the turn of the century, the most recent documented threats have been largely factors affecting hydrology and water quality - impoundments and channelization, siltation, and pollution. Loss of fish hosts necessary for reproduction has also been a problem. Recent research carried out under the auspices of the IUCN/SSC Trade Specialist Group points to an additional potential threat - over-exploitation for use in the cultured pearl industry.

The unionid fauna of the United States currently provide the sole seed material for the World's cultured pearl industry, which extends far beyond Japan to other parts of Asia and the Pacific, including Australia, Indonesia, Korea, Papua New Guinea, the Pilippines, Taiwan, and Thailand. Since 1983, black pearls have been French Polynesia's leading export commodity: according to the Tahitian Ministere de la Mer, the roughly 500 Kg of black pearls exported in 1988 were estimated to value almost US $23 million.

Preliminary results of a review of U.S. Fish and Wildlife Service and other trade data indicate minimum exports of raw Unionid shell averaging between 5,000 and 6,000 tonnes per year since 1986, a dramatic increase over previous levels dating as far back as the late 1960's. Japan continues to be the predominant importer, as it is almost exclusively Japanese technicians that manufacture the shell beads or 'blanks' for implantation into pearl oysters for culturing.

While commercial musseling employs a few thousand fishermen in the United States, the number of commercial mussel exporters is limited to seven or eight companies and the number of documented importers to fewer than twenty. No more than six countries have been reported as importing raw shell from the U.S. The number of species identified in trade is similarly small: **Megalonaias nervosa** is by far the predominant species exported; others include **Amblema plicata, Fusconaia ebena, Pleurobema cordatum, Quadrula pustulosa**, and **Quadrula quadrula**.

Although export documents might suggest that the harvest of Unionids is limited to only a few, generally common species, the nature of the harvest virtually ensures that protected species are taken incidentally wherever their ranges overlap with commercial activity. Murky water and non-selective gear are the major factors responsible for this incidental take, which not only threatens the survival of a number of endangered species but also substantial volumes of non-target species and specimens of no commercial value. Steve Ahlstedt of the Tennessee Valley Authority, one of the world's experts on U.S. Unionids, has estimated that as many as fifteen tons of mussels may be harvested and killed to yield one ton of mussels for commercial export value.

While the incidental take of protected species in the commercial harvest is obviously cause for concern, the sheer volume of the mussel harvest, particularly in light of Ahlstedt's assertion, and past history of over-exploitation of the environmentally sensitive animals raises equally compelling questions regarding the sustainability of harvest levels and survivability of mussel populations. An apparent consensus amongst malacologists and fisheries biologists most familiar with these species that they are being heavily over-exploited has not yet translated into effective management at either the state or federal level, and additional harvest and trade controls and population monitoring programs are considered essential to ensuring the long-term viability of the species' populations. These programs will become increasingly necessary as the pearl industry further expands in Asia and the Pacific, for until experimentation with synthetic nuclei yields positive results, this industry will continue to be dependent on this rapidly disappearing U.S. resource.

Natural pearls do still occur in the United States, as shown in the following note by Steven McCormack describing a visit to the United States of America by Scottish pearl fishers in 1990.

We arrived in New York excited but tired by our journey. The airline's microwaved cuisine washed down by several large Jack Daniels had not helped during the last turbulent hop from Boston to La Guardia.

That morning we had left Prestwick basking in the Scottish equivalent of a heat wave, three days of unbroken sunshine, but eleven hours later and an ocean away 'The Big Apple' was bobbing around in the wettest May since records began.

After a couple of days' acclimatisation at the home of a relative in Connecticut, we made our way North, to up state New York, past the state capital Albany and on through the beautiful Adirondack mountains, by the pine covered shores of Lakes Placid and Saranac and beyond to St. Lawrence county and the tiny settlement of South Russel.

The family we were to live with for the next twelve days lived on Silver Hill, where in the last century a small silver mine had prospered for a time and then petered out, leaving only a dirt road, a few wooden houses and a name.

After an enthusiastic welcome from our hosts we settled in for the night, full of anticipation of what the morning's fishing might bring. I remembered the story of how a man named Nathaniel Higgins had found a pearl of sixty Troy grains in the nearby Grasse River and dreamt of emulating him.

The next day, replete with bacon, eggs, pancakes and maple syrup, we set off for Plumb Brook, a small tributary of the Grasse River, which ran just a few hundred yards from the house. The Goodwin brothers, Peter and Jeremy, would take the van upstream, whilst my uncle Donald, young Donald and I would make our way on foot downstream. We hadn't gone far when we reached what could only be described as a swamp with the brook meandering through it. I had little faith in this muddy thicket of bushes and Thorny Apple trees, but my uncle assured me that they (the mussels) were in there.

We were only in the water a few minutes when we started to find the odd mussel; soon they were abundant, but not quite as abundant as the clouds of mosquitoes and Deer-fly which were busy devouring or attempting to devour every area of unprotected skin they could find. We fished for several hours checking and marking each shell before returning it to the water. After examining several bags full to no avail, I began to feel slightly disheartened, when on the other side of a rock sat a large cluster of mussels embedded in a deposit of fine clay. I knew that if I disturbed the bottom I would make the water too cloudy to see them, so I did what all good pearl fishers do at a time like this: I opted for the most promising shell. They were all large and healthy, but one gave a faint impression of having a 'turn in the nose' - a slight distortion of the top of the mussel. So, after carefully retrieving it from the bottom, I held it up to show my uncle who, with his expert eye, immediately pronounced 'There's a big pearl in that one, I can see it through the gap in the hinge'.

Sure enough, inside I found a beautiful milky-white pearl of approx. twenty troy grains. I could hardly contain myself, but this was just the first of several large pearls we were to find in the days ahead.

The river was unlike any other river we had fished. There were very few small mussels, practically no mussels in deep water, and a distinct lack of 'Crooks', the much sought after malformed shells often found to be pearl bearing. Also, those pearls we did get, though of large size and excellent quality, were not accompanied by the usual numbers of smaller pearls. Some days a man could fish all day without so much as a seed pearl to show for it, then the next day he might find something in excess of ten grains.

As the days went by, the fishing became more and more arduous as we ventured into the more inaccessible reaches of the river. At times it seemed as though every thorn was out to impale you and every sanguivorous winged insect on Gods earth was determined to have a picnic at your expense. However, by the end of the trip we had made enough money to cover ourselves, made many new friends and made this third trip to North America an overwhelming success.

The above account not only gives us an insight into a pearl fisher's excitement and enjoyment during the 'chase', but also emphasises just how much the world has shrunk in the last fifty years, making conservation controls all the more difficult to enforce.

CONSERVATION

Invertebrates represent more than 80% of Europe's animal life, but the sheer number of invertebrate species, or indeed those of a single species, do not safeguard their survival as evidenced by the current status of the pearl mussel considered here. The main reasons for this decline can be attributed to the destruction and/or deterioration of its habitat as a direct result of man's activities such as pollution and acidification of watercourses, uncontrolled activities of pearl fishing, changes to the natural hydrological system of watercourses by hydroelectric schemes, fish farming, drainage schemes and artificial canalisation, etc., examples of which follow.

Attention was first draw to the effects road development may have on mussel populations by the following note in *Science Gossip* for January 1873:

It is a popular theory in Scotland "that the building of bridges diminishes the number of pearls in the rivers." May not this be that before the bridges were built, the cattle in fording the streams trod upon the mussels and the injury done to the shell caused the formation of pearls. When the cattle cross by the bridges the secretion is no longer promoted in this way.

The Scottish observers were correct in their supposition which no doubt arose from personal experience, especially amongst pearl fishers. The explanation given for this reduction as being due to transferring the cattle over the river via a bridge instead of through it at a ford would undoubtedly lessen pearl mussel shells becoming damaged, but this would be negligible upon the production of pearls. However, bridge building would certainly have a direct effect on mussel populations due to disruption and modification of the river banks adjacent to and immediately upstream of the bridge during its construction. In addition, this construction process affects the entire river levels, disturbance of the river bottom resulting in excess sediment in suspension, etc. Long term effects may also result due to alterations to the river course at the bridge site, for example bridge piles, the straightening or deepening of the river channel immediately beneath the bridge, etc., such modifications often resulting in changes to the water flow further downstream. Now, as we approach the twenty-first century, these pressures are further increased through the run-off waters from roads and bridges containing pollutants, coupled with improved drainage channels, the straightening of river courses, etc.

Donald Brown MacCulloch refers to the consequences of these activities on Glen Spean in his 1947 *Prince Charlie's Country and its neighbouring Clan Lands* thus:

> The main road and railway which wind throughout the glen do not in the least mar its scenery but the construction of the dams at Loch Treig and Loch Luggan by the Hydro-electric Company has almost dried up the River Spean which used to be a roaring torrent in a deep and rugged gorge.

Again in the preface to the 2nd (1948) edition of his *Romantic Lochaber*, MacCulloch writes:

> A great deal of timber-felling was carried out during the war in the rich woodlands of the district which has altered to a great extent many of its features, unfortunately not to their scenic benefit.

This highlights the major changes in land use by agriculture, including fish-farming, and forestry, all of which rely heavily on improved land drainage, chemical fertilisers, mechanisation, etc.

An idea of the immense devastation through a combination of the above activities may be gained from the following account by A. E. Boycott and E.

W. Bowell concerning pearl mussel population in the river Wye, Herefordshire. These were published in the Transaction of the *Woolhope Naturalists' Field Club* for 1900:

Very abundant in the Wye round Hereford and elsewhere, at Whitchurch, etc. Empty valves may be found on almost every gravel beach, and the live shell is easy to obtain. It is nearly always badly eroded, and always small. Specimens from Brunton are in some cases eroded right through the shell: sand, etc., then enters the hole, but this is soon skinned over by the Mollusc, and consequently a hard mass - frequently of considerable size - of agglutinated sand and mucus material is to be found blocking the hole. Various stages in the process may be seen; from the case where the sand has merely a skin between it and the snail, to examples whose shells shew on their interior hard lumps in which the sand is thoroughly impregnated and bound together with secretion. It is in the last degree unlikely that these examples of perforated shells are due to fracture rather than erosion.

It lives in the rapid part of the Wye, where there is a more or less sandy bottom, in from 1.5 to 4 or 5 feet of water: it seems to prefer a depth of about 3 feet. Deep holes and muddy localities with but a sluggish stream of water it does not seem to affect much. It is often found in especial abundance in the shoal water at the head of rapids, where the bottom consists of fairly large stones, the interstices being filled with sand and fine gravel. For instance, we have taken it in great plenty just above the Castle Green ferry at Hereford, on the Bullinghope side, and also just above a rapid near Brunton. It is easier taken in the early part of the year (March, April), when it moves into quite shallow water near the bank. At such times they may be seen crowding the beds of the little sandy bays which often occur at the foot of a beach. Here they move about freely, and their long, curving tracks are very conspicuous on the bottom. It often walks in a very nearly regular circle, and we should judge, from various data, that from 12 - 15 feet in a day would be an average journey. When not moving, it resumes its almost vertical posture, or at any rate sinks deeper into the sand: the marks of these stoppages may be seen on their tracks. We have noticed precisely similar phenomena in **Anodonta** and **Unio pictorum**. It does not bury so much of its shell in the soil as e.g. **A. cygnea**: this is very possibly correlated with the usually hard bottom in which **M. margaritifera** occurs.'

How different the picture now, some ninety years later, since, in the summer of 1992, colleagues from the National Museum of Wales at Cardiff, undertook an intensive survey of the entire River Wye from its source down to its junction with the River Severn during which they found less than thirty living individuals of **Margaritifera,** aged forty years or more, in the entire length of the River.

Sadly, the above observations on the River Wye prove to be the norm, not only in Britain but throughout the whole of the pearl mussels range. For this reason, considerable discussion has taken place in the last five or six years in an effort to protect not only this species, but its freshwater habitat, together with all the associated animals and plants, from total extinction. A brief outline of this activity, including the resultant British and European legislation, follows, in order to draw it to the notice of Landowners, Local Authorities, the general public, and law enforcers alike.

NATURALLY

CAIRNCROSS
— of PERTH ·—

Home to a unique collection of Scottish river pearls,
exquisitely crafted for individually designed settings.

18 St John Street, Perth 0738 24367

EST
1869

Send for our complimentary brochure.

PROTECTIVE LEGISLATION

In September 1986, Edinburgh hosted the Ninth International Malacological Congress during which informal discussion ensued concerning the dramatic decline of the freshwater pearl mussel, **Margaritifera margaritifera** (Linnaeus). As a result the author, in conjunction with the Biological Recording in Scotland Campaign, The Scottish Wildlife Trust, and Glasgow Museums, set up, with financial assistance from the Worldwide Fund for Nature, an initial three year survey of this species in Scotland. This was launched on 11th January 1989 and has provided information on the present distribution of this species together with an insight into the factors contributing to its decline such as road developments, forestation, changing agricultural practices, fish-farming, hydro-electric schemes, peat extraction and the pet and gardening trades. Attention was also drawn to the problems arising from the activities of irresponsible and uncontrolled exploitation by amateur pearl fishers searching for mythical fortunes. Professional pearlfishing has provided an additional means of livelihood to Scottish rural communities since Roman times and, provided it is carried out correctly, should not cause undue detriment to the mussel populations concerned. For this reason traditional Scottish pearlfishers assisted in drawing up draft regulations to allow them to continue their traditional craft, at the same time ensuring the future conservation of the pearl mussel stocks. The resultant draft **Proposals for licencing pearl fishing** were first presented to the Tenth International Malacological Congress at Tubingen, Germany in September 1989 in the hope that they would form a basis for future legislation to safeguard Scotland's natural and cultural heritage.

At this time, 1989, pearl fishing was banned in continental Europe, whilst in Northern Ireland the Pearl Mussel is protected through **The Wildlife (Northern Ireland) Order 1985**, Statutory Instruments 1985 No. 171 (N.I. 2) under section 1: **Sale, etc. of live or dead wild animals** which states:

13 (1). Subject to the provisions of this Part, if any person -

> a. sells or offers or exposes for sale, or has in his possession or transports or causes to be transported for the purpose of sale at any premises any live wild animal included in Schedule 7:

> b. publishes or causes to be published any advertisement likely to be understood as conveying that he buys or sells, or intends to buy or sell, any such animal,

he shall be guilty of an offence.

(2) Subject to the provisions of this Part, if any person who is not for the time being registered in accordance with regulations made by the Department -

> a. sells, offers or exposes for sale, or has in his possession or transports or causes to be transported for the purpose of sale at any premises any dead wild animal included in Schedule 7 or any part, or anything derived from, such a wild animal; or

> b. publishes or causes to be published any advertisement likely to be understood as conveying that he buys or sells, or intends to buy or sell, any of those things,

he shall be guilty of an offence.

(Schedule 7)

Schedule 7
Animals which may not be sold dead or alive at any time

Common name	Scientific name
Mussel, Freshwater	**Margaritifera margaritifera**

NOTE. The first column of this Schedule, which gives the common name or names, is included by way of guidance only; in the event of any dispute or proceedings only the second column is to be taken into account.

From the above it is apparent that not only is it illegal to deal in live or dead pearl mussels, **Margaritifera margaritifera (in Northern Ireland)**, but also anything derived from them thus it would appear illegal to buy or sell pearls unless registered with the appropriate Department to do so.

Limited protection was further afforded in March 1988 with the enlargement of the appendices to the 1979 Bern Convention of European Wildlife and Natural Habitats to include invertebrates with the result that **Margaritifera auricularia** (Spengler), which now occurs in Spain, was added to Annex II, that is a species which is strictly protected together with its habitat.

At the same time three further freshwater mussel species, **Unio elongatulus** C. Pfeiffer, **Microcondylaea compressa** (Menke) and **Margaritifera margaritifera** (Linnaeus) were added to Annex III, that is, species whose exploitation should be the subject of a management plan.

In November 1989 the author reported further on observations obtained from the Scottish survey under the title *Problems in the control of exploitation of freshwater mussels, with particular reference to Margaritifera* to the Colloquy on the Bern Convention invertebrates and their conservation, organised by the European Invertebrate Survey and the Council of

Europe and which was held at Strasbourg. Attention was drawn to the problems involved through attempting to legislate for Margaritifera in isolation from other Unionids. At the conclusion of the Colloquy it was suggested that the Standing Committee to the Bern Convention set up a group of experts on Bern Convention invertebrates (BCIs) with the following terms of reference:

1. Gather old and new information BCIs setting up a project with EIS, to compile these data into species data sheets which will seek to:

   a. revise the status of BCIs;

   b. propose precise conservation action to be carried out for BCIs;

   c. produce inventories of BCIs in national parks and other protected sites of known international importance to conservation;

   d. identify sites of special interest for the conservation of BCIs;

2. Identify priorities in relation to protection of BCIs, based on information derived from data sheet production;

3. Suggest studies on habitats of especial importance for European Invertebrates;

4. Follow progress on invertebrates conservation in Contracting Parties (including EEC efforts);

5. Suggest amendments to the Appendices (long term task), consulting with EIS and other bodies to this end;

6. Elaborate lists of sites of special invertebrate interest;

7. Discuss ways of co-ordinating efforts for conservation of transborder populations of BCIs;

8. Suggest legislative mechanisms potentially appropriate for conservation of invertebrates, for consideration by national governments;

9. Prepare for the attention of the Standing Committee recommendations to Contracting Parties concerning different aspects of invertebrate conservation;

10. Seek to identify mechanisms for promoting and popularising invertebrates and their conservation;

11. Other items of invertebrate conservation concern;

12. Report periodically to the Standing Committee of the Convention.

A group of experts on conservation of invertebrates with the above terms of reference was created by the Standing Committee to the Bern Convention on the 8th December 1989. The first meeting of this Group of Experts was held at Strasbourg from 23-25 April 1990 where the author presented a data sheet on **Margaritifera margaritifera** together with draft proposals for legislation. These formed the basis for the following recommendation which was submitted by the Group of Experts to the Standing Committee for their consideration. These proposals were adopted on 11 January 1991 by the Standing Committee of the Convention on the Conservation of European Wildlife and Natural Habitats and are:

Recommendation No. 22 on the conservation of the pearl mussel **(Margaritifera margaritifera)** and other freshwater mussels (Unionoida).

Noting that the number of **Margaritifera margaritifera** is rapidly decreasing in the territories of most of the states which are Contracting Parties to the convention, mainly as a result of pollution and acidification of water courses, uncontrolled activities of pearl fishing, alteration of the natural hydrological system of water courses by hydroelectric schemes, fish farming, drainage schemes and artificial canalisation:

Considering that all Unionoida need to receive greater conservation attention as many of the species of the group are in decline:

Noting that the freshwater form of the pearl mussel **(Margaritifera margaritifera durrovensis)** has sharply declined and is under particular threat from pollution:

Considering that, to manage their populations, more factual information on the biology and distribution of freshwater mussels is required,

Recommends that Contracting Parties;

1.   regulate or prohibit the exploitation of freshwater mussels, including where necessary the establishment of licences for pearl fishers of **Margaritifera margaritifera** and the regulation of recreational and research collecting;

2.   regulate the sale and transport of native freshwater mussels, as appropriate, and the introduction of non-native species;

3.   consider the establishment of special mussel reserves;

4.   evaluate the impact of tourism, road development and pollution, in particular by silt from peatbog stripping, on freshwater mussel populations;

5.   carry out environmental impact assessment prior to the installation of fish farms, taking into account important mussel populations;

6.   encourage research on all aspects of the biology and geographical distribution of freshwater mussels,

including the realisation of surveys to locate important mussel populations;

7. promote co-ordination at national and international level of survey and research programmes on freshwater mussels, with the eventual establishment of co-ordinating centres and data banks, in conjunction with the European Invertebrate Survey;

8. investigate the commercial viability of mussel cultivation for food, water filtration and purification, medicinal use, environmental monitoring and pearl production;

9. consider the need to establish breeding and reintroduction programmes for threatened freshwater mussels.

The above recommendation encompasses the majority of points raised at the 1989 Bern Colloquium as well as enlarging the protection to include all freshwater mussels (Unionoida). At this 1990 Group of Experts meeting it was also decided that the author should prepare draft proposals to amend Appendix IV of the Bern Convention (prohibited means and methods of killing, capture and other forms of exploitation) expressly for Unionids for consideration by the group at their next meeting in 1992 . .

On the 27th March 1991 **Margaritifera** gained limited protection throughout Great Britain through the introduction of a variation to the Wildlife and Country side Act as follows:

Wildlife and Countryside Act 1981 (Variation of Schedule) Order 1991 No. 367.

(Variation of Schedule 5)

Variation of Schedule 5

2. (3) The freshwater pearl mussel (**Margaritifera margaritifera**) is hereby added to Schedule 5 to the Act, but only in respect of section 9(1) so far as it relates to killing and injuring.

Section 9(1) of the 1981 Wildlife and Countryside Act states:

9. (1) Subject to the provisions of this Part, if any person intentionally kills, injures or takes any wild animal included in Schedule 5, he shall be guilty of an offence.

(6) In any proceedings for an offence under subsection (1), (2) or (5)(a), the animal in question shall be presumed to have been a wild animal unless the contrary is shown.

Whilst Section 10 covers possible exception under

10. (3) Notwithstanding anything in section 9, a person shall not be guilty of an offence by reason of -

(a) the taking of any such animal if he shows that the animal had been disabled otherwise than by his unlawful act and was taken solely for the purpose of tending it and releasing it when no longer disabled;

(b) the killing of any such animal if he shows that the animal had been so seriously disabled otherwise than by his unlawful act that there was no reasonable chance of its recovering; or

(c) any act made unlawful by that section if he shows that the act was the incidental result of a lawful operation and could not reasonably have been avoided.

(4) Notwithstanding anything in section 9, an authorised person shall not be guilty of an offence by reason of the killing or injuring of a wild animal included in Schedule 5 if he shows that his action was necessary for the purpose of preventing serious damage to livestock, foodstuffs for livestock, crops, vegetables, fruit, growing timber or any other form of property or fisheries.

(6) An authorised person shall not be entitled to rely on the defence provided by subsection (4) as respects any action taken at any time if it had become apparent, before that time, that that action would prove necessary for the purpose mentioned in that subsection and either -

(a) a licence under section 16 authorising that action had not been applied for as soon as reasonably practicable after that fact had become apparent; or

(b) an application for such a licence had been determined.

1991 also saw the signing of the Habitat and Species Directive at Maastrich. This was produced by the European Community at Brussels and aims at the protection of natural and semi-natural habitats and their fauna and flora. The Directive appendices include the following Unionoida species:

Unionidae	Appendix
Microcondylaea compressa (Menke)	V
Unio crassus (Philippson)	II & IV
Unio elongatulus C. Pfeiffer	V

Margaritiferidae	
Margaritifera auricularia (Spengler)	IV
Margaritifera margaritifera (Linnaeus)	II & V

Appendix II species of which the habitat should be protected.

Appendix IV strictly protected species.

Appendix V species the exploitation of which should be the subject of a management plan.

The Group of Experts on Conservation of Invertebrates met again at Strasbourg in March 1992 and produced the following proposals, based on a draft prepared by the author, concerning *Prohibited means of capture or exploitation of Unionids*. These were submitted to the Standing Committee of the Convention on the Conservation of European Wildlife and Natural Habitats in December 1992:

Recalling that **Margaritifera margaritifera** is a protected species included in Appendix III to the convention;

Recalling its Recommendation no. 22 (91) on the conservation of the pearl mussel **(Margaritifera margaritifera)** and other freshwater mussels (Unionoida);

Noting that the number of **Margaritifera margaritifera** is rapidly decreasing in the territories of most of the states which are Contracting Parties to the Convention, mainly as a result of pollution and acidification of watercourses, uncontrolled activities of pearl fishing, alteration of the natural hydrological system of watercourses by hydroelectric schemes, fish farming, drainage schemes and artificial canalisation;

Recommend that Contracting Parties:

Regulate as appropriate the licensing of pearl fishing and the taking of **Margaritifera margaritifera**, establishing in particular:

- a list of authorised methods of pearl fishing,
- a minimum size of pearl mussel,
- prohibition of fishing outside the hours of daylight,
- a code of practice for pearl fishing based on the suggestions made in the appendix to this recommendation.

APPENDIX TO THE RECOMMENDATION

1. The pearl mussel will not be killed, injured or harmed in any way

2. The adductor muscle will not be over-stretched or torn whilst an inspection is taking place

3. Only officially approved opening tongs with a maximum opening of 1.0 cm and designed to cause minimum damage to the animal tissue/shell of the mussel will be used, extreme care being exercised to ensure that the mussel is opened slowly. The amount of opening should relate to the size and age of the mussel

4. Pearl mussels will be returned alive and unharmed to the water at their original site after inspection or removal of pearls. They will not be removed and placed elsewhere

5. There will be no taking or possessing of pearl mussels under the size of 8 cm.

6. Where practicable mussels from which pearls have been removed will be marked before returning to the river to prevent future unnecessary handling

7. The following "TRADITIONAL" methods of pearl fishing will be used:-

   a/ From the shore, namely by wading, using glass-bottomed viewing device and traditional cleft stick b/ From a boat, using a glass-bottomed viewing device and traditional cleft stick

8. Pearl fishing must be practised during the hours of daylight only

9. Pearls collected during the season will be disposed of through an officially approved outlet. An annual record of such transactions will be kept and available for inspection by the licencing body to allow for future assessment of the industry

10. Local regulations and conditions may be imposed in the interests of conservation of Margaritifera and other Unionids by the appropriate authority in each country dependent upon current conditions:- e.g. pollution, run down stock, re-introduction to improved habitat, official close season etc and it is the licencee's responsibility to be fully conversant with and abide by such regulations pertaining to the area in which he is operating.

As time progresses it is expected further protection will be afforded through legislative controls in regard to industrial development, agricultural practices, etc. coupled with an increase in general awareness of the importance of safeguarding our natural environment.

THE FUTURE

To many the future seems bleak; and total extinction seemingly inevitable, bearing in mind the dramatic decline of pearl mussel populations throughout the whole of its former range. This is understandable when one considers that **Margaritifera** represents possibly the longest living, most widely distributed and greatest numerically represented multicellular invertebrate that has ever inhabited the freshwater environment. Hopefully, all is not lost, however, since the species' extreme longevity coupled with its considerable ability to withstand adverse conditions by means of closing up and going into torpor provide us with a life-line by which we may be enabled to sustain this remarkable species.

In recent years, considerable progress has been achieved in the restoration of extremely polluted rivers to their former water quality. For example, the River Clyde has suffered extreme deterioration in water quality through the direct effects of intense industrialisation, modifications to its water channels and agricultural residual pollutants. This activity had become so bad that in the early 1960's anyone falling in was almost certain to be suffocated due to a lack of oxygen in the air immediately above the river surface. The water sustained little or no animal life, the salmon, which had been so plentiful in this river in the late eighteenth and early nineteenth century being completely absent. Due to public concern the local authorities set about trying to rectify the situation, with such success that by the early 1980's salmon were beginning, once more, to pass up the Clyde to the spawning grounds in its upper reaches. This has been coupled with considerable recolonisation of other freshwater vertebrates and invertebrates. It would seem reasonable to hope that this process will continue and that in due course conditions will become favourable for recolonisation by mussel populations, hopefully for relict stock which may as yet survive undetected in the upper reaches and feeder streams, or by intentional restocking from populations as near to the Clyde stock as practicable.

In this connection, considerable research has been carried out in the last ten years, on propagating mussels by replacing the parasitic glochidial phase on a fish through the use of an artificial medium in the laboratory. These trials are still at an early stage, but it has been possible to raise some species on a chemically impregnated agar jelly, providing traces of fish blood are present. This stimulates the glochidia to undergo metamorphosis to produce a juvenile mussel, so that once this method is perfected it should be possible to raise a maximum number of juveniles from a limited number of mussels. Indeed, since the pearl mussel is capable of self-fertilization in extreme conditions and each mussel produces around two million glochidia each breeding season, it would be feasible to obtain several thousand mussels from a single individual per season, if so desired. In ideal natural conditions, the number of juveniles reaching the post fish stage would probably total up to a maximum of ten individuals at the most for each mussel, but in most years two or three down to none.

In Germany parallel propagation work has been carried out by infecting trout and salmon fingerlings in fish-farms with glochidia and then releasing the infected fish into the natural habitat. This method has also proved successful. Hence, once the rivers become returned to their former condition pearl mussel populations may once again colonise suitable habitats.

Sadly, our interpretation of what constitutes a pristine freshwater habitat is clouded by the fact that the majority of European rivers have been considerably modified and downgraded by human activity during the past two hundred years. Until the break-up of the former Soviet Union our standard bench mark was considerably below the conditions prevalent in European rivers even as late as the middle of the last century. In 1992, however, I had the good fortune to be invited by my Russian colleagues to accompany them to see at first hand what may be one of the most pristine natural pearl mussel populations in the world. This occurs in the Varzuga River on the Kola Peninsula and is worth mentioning in more detail.

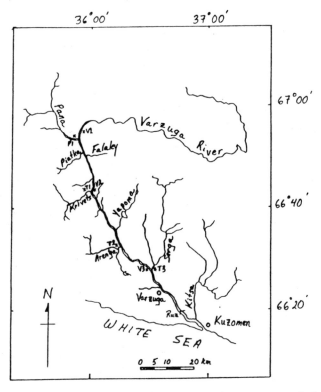

Best we could do for a map of the Varzuga River system; nobody Moscow seemed to have one and most Western atlases degenerate into unnamed wild artistic blue squiggles.

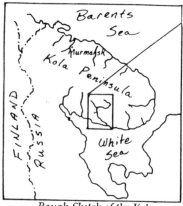

Rough Sketch of the Kola,
Varzuga R. in box

I arrived at Moscow at the beginning of August and travelled by train to Kandalaksha, a journey of two days confined to a four berth carriage. From Kandalaksha we then continued by bus over rough, untarmacked roads to Umba village, the administrative capital of the Tersky District. Umba, with a population of about 9,000, is situated on the White Sea and is an active sea port.

The sparsely populated Kola Peninsula of Northern Russia is largely situated within the Arctic circle, being bounded to the north by the Barents Sea and to the south by the White Sea. As a result the climatic conditions are relatively extreme: summer temperatures at the beginning of my visit being in the mid seventies, but already falling at night to freezing by the first week in September and continuing down to minus 30 or more in the winter months. This somewhat inhospitable climate helps to account for the sparse human population which is predominantly situated along the coastal areas. In addition, this area was off-limits until 1991 to most visitors, including Russians, due to its military importance both as a base and source of mineral resources. As a direct result, the area exhibits a contradictory mosaic of virtually pristine natural environments, interspersed with areas of extreme industrial pollution producedby massive heavy industries, uncontrolled mineral extraction, strategic naval bases and military testing area.

Umba provided our base camp at the local fish hatchery, where salmon were reared in large, shallow, concrete tanks, which have a gravity-fed water supply from the Umba River. The eggs used are obtained from fish caught from the Umba River in traps at Umba and also in the larger trap, which completely blocks the river, several miles upstream. Some of the eggs obtained here are sent to a further hatchery at Kandalaksha for enhancement programmes on other Russian rivers. The fingerlings raised at Umba hatchery are subsequently released, normally when about two years old but depending on body weight, back into the Umba, but some surplus stock is also introduced into other rivers in the area. The main aim of this process is to conserve the fish populations in these rivers, but affords little consideration for maintaining the genetic strains of the individual populations. In the long term such actions may well prove detrimental, if experience of similar populations in Western Europe prevail.

The Umba hatchery have generously provided laboratory facilities for further research on the interactions between salmon and pearl mussels and it is here that the early experiments on infecting fingerling salmon with pearl mussel glochidia obtained from the Varzuga mussel populations are being undertaken.

From Umba we then flew by helicopter to the junction of the Pana and Indol Rivers, a distance of about 170 kilometres, to begin our journey rafting down the Varzuga to Varzuga village.

Flying over this Arctic wilderness, one could only marvel at the extensive patchwork of upright stands of Silver Birch and Scots Pine, separated by a seemingly endless network of waterways and large expanses of Bilberry and Reindeer-moss covered open spaces. Give or take the odd roaming herd of larger mammals and the ground down stumps of mountains, one has a pretty fair impression of much of northern Britain before the hand of man.

The only evidence of life was the occasional small herd of reindeer and the floating logs of timber advertising mans presence. In places these logs had become jammed together, posing a future hazard to the environment through resultant flooding and modification to the water courses. These indiscriminate logging activities are directly responsible for observed ecological and erosional problems at the felling sites, such as soil removal and the loss of specific habitats. In addition, such deforestation affords a considerably underestimated threat to the aquatic fauna and flora in the drainage area through releasing toxins present in the tree sap. In several locations considerable white, foam-like accumulations were to be seen, which most probably arose through this process.

The Varzuga River drains into the White Sea and is considered to be one of the most productive Atlantic salmon rivers in the world, with an estimated 50,000 to 70,000 Atlantic salmon ascending the river annually. It also contains one of the largest populations of the Pearl Mussel, **Margaritifera margaritifera** (Linnaeus 1758), whose numbers are estimated to be in excess of 50 million. These are distributed over some 220 kilometres of the river, being present in the deeper water near midstream. Unlike Scottish populations, they are apparently absent for about ten metres from the shore. This, possibly, is due to their being unable to survive in this area in the winter months due to the severe ice conditions which prevail from mid October to May. The river is completely frozen over during this period, whilst ice scour marks, commonly to be seen on trees adjacent to the river, indicate its extent and severity.

On arrival at the Indol-Pana junction, we set up camp and searched the scrub for mushrooms and berries for our first meal. This consisted of mushroom soup, salmon from the river, washed down with Bilberry tea, (Bilberries boiled in water from the river!). The first impressions of such a meal were excellent, but eleven days of the same fare, regardless of substituting grayling for salmon and two lots of duck soup, tended to deaden its culinary delights.

The next task was to assemble our catamaran, which consisted of two air-filled canvas floats connected by means of tubular metal rods. These were covered by pieces of nylon netting to form a platform, to which we fastened our belongings, protected in polythene sheeting, and used as a seat for the ensuing journey.

Before breaking camp we visited a large pearl mussel colony on the Indol, which was situated about three kilometres upstream. Here the river was about forty metres wide, fairly slow moving, with the mussels in depths varying from one to three metres in the mid-stream section. One of my Russian colleagues, Dr. Ziuganov, swam to the middle of the river in his wet suit and proceeded to scan the river bed through a 'Japanese Eye', which consisted of an oval fibre-glass box with the base made of perspex to provide a viewing window. This device, he assured me, was the sort used by Japanese pearl divers to examine the sea-bed in search of the marine pearl oyster, **Pinctada.** On spotting a group of freshwater pearl mussels, my colleague dove to the bottom to collect them by hand. This technique was necessary due to the depth at which they occurred, but had the disadvantage that such a method produces agitation of the mud and sand on the river bed resulting in a loss of visibility.

The mussels obtained varied in size. Adults, on average, were about five inches, down to juveniles of around a year in age. These were attached to the larger adult members in the colony by means of a single byssal thread. Their shells measured about 8 millimetres in length, whereas the byssal threads were in the region of two centimetres. This is the first and only time that I have observed juveniles with byssal threads in the wild, although Neil McCormack informs me he used to see them fairly frequently in Scottish populations in years gone by, but that now they are of rare occurrence. In the present case there were several, although we only spent about twenty minutes collecting since we required fifty individuals for future research to be undertaken at Umba.

The other significant observation, for me, was to note the considerable number of small associated organisms present, which appeared to be an intimate component of the pearl mussel colony. My Russian companion, Dr. Ziuganov, had already proposed the hypothesis that the reason why the Varzuga river is such a good salmon river is due to the presence of the large pearl mussel population. He suggests that the mussel population maintains the cleanliness of the water, since each mussel filters up to thirty litres of water per day. He suggests that this resultant clean water, devoid of excessive organic debris, proves highly suitable for the development of salmon fry in the extensive salmon spawning grounds sited in the Varzuga river system. This is presumably due to the minimal loss of salmon eggs through fungal infection. He points out that such a dense annual production of salmon fry in turn benefits the pearl mussel populations due to providing abundant suitable fish hosts for the mussels' parasitic glochidial stage. My personal observations during the trip fully support his claims, but I would also suggest that the pristine state of the mussel populations, with their inter-dependent fauna and flora, provide an abundant microscopic food supply for the developing salmon fry during their early development stages. It should also be noted that in addition to pearl mussels, the rivers support immense populations of smaller bivalves belonging to the orb shells, **Sphaerium,** which, in places, appeared like handfuls of puffed wheat. These too actively filter the waters to maintain their clarity, affording another food source to larger fish, such as trout.

Returning, we then broke camp and rafted down the Pana to its junction with the Varzuga. Passing through some of the most beautiful scenery imaginable; the river banks clothed with stands of Scots Pine, Spruce, Poplar, Birch and Aspen, separated by more open boggy areas of Bilberries and Cranberries, Blueberries and Willow Herb. Also, a rich ground cover of horsetails, lichens, mosses and ferns, whilst fungi abounded aplenty.

From here to the mouth of the Pana, the river is comprised of a series of deep, slow runs and pools, flowing over solid bedrock, boulders and sand with characteristic aquatic plants such as **Potamogeton** and **Ranunculus** with occasional clumps of Water Lilies present in the quieter bays of the larger pools.

We landed just upstream of the Pana-Varzuga junction, where the fairly steep three metre high bank made the task of dragging the catamarans up rather arduous. Even in this remote isolated region the small flattened area suitable for our campsite was littered with empty tin cans, fragments of nylon netting, etc., evidently used by salmon poachers. We have a lot to answer for!

Before continuing downstream we surveyed the mussel colony present in mid-stream and obtained numerous large individuals, if anything bigger than those in the Indol, again with juveniles attached by their byssal threads.

Below the Pana junction, down to the Piatka and Falaley tributaries, the river becomes wider and more shallow, with more riffles and exposed gravel banks, Dr. Ziuganov informed me, provided important salmon spawning grounds.

Immediately below the inflow of the Piatka and Falaley tributaries the river is badly discoloured as a result of material in suspension being brought down off the marshy areas. An apparent effect of this material in suspension was the total absence of pearl mussels for a distance of about one hundred metres below the inflow, this phenomena being present at all the tributary inflows observed as we travelled downstream.

Below the Falaley to Krivets the river consists of a fairly long stretch with depths in the region of two or more metres, flowing between its raised banks, some four metres high, covered by mixed Pine, Spruce and Silver Birch. The river surface was broken from time to time by large, irregular, tooth-like boulders protruding above the surface; the river, this year, according to Dr. Ziuganov, being considerably higher than the previous year.

At Krivets the river consisted of more frequent riffle and minor rapids, alternating with long, deep runs where the river passed between solid rock outcrops. The river banks here afforded numerous dead shells washed out during periods of spate, the pearl mussel colony in this area being considerable.

Further downstream, at Yapoma, the river widens to over 150 metres whilst the bottom deposits become more sandy, pearl mussels again being present in numbers. Next, the Arenaga, which has an impressive waterfall with a height of about fifteen metres situated some three kilometres upstream. This acts as a natural barrier to migrating salmon stocks which are apparently absent above it. Below Arenaga the river gradient continues to increase as the river narrows once more to pass between the vertically high cliffs of exposed bedrock. In this region the river alternates between long, deep, medium flowing stretches and fast flowing rapids, such as the Sukhoy Iovas Rapid. These vary in depth and severity, but were readily navigable in our canvas catamarans which, being partly inflated, tended to give as they slid over the waterworn rock surfaces. Had they been of manufactured western design and made of rubber, it is highly probable they would have broken under the onslaught.

Further downstream, in the region of Punz Ostrov Island, which is about three kilometres above the Serga inflow, the river again widens to about 150 metres, the resulting decrease in velocity producing numerous riffles and sand and gravel bars, whilst the shorelines are of sand and rounded cobbles. Mussels are again relatively plentiful in this region extending downstream to two or three kilometres above Varzuga village, where they become scarce. This is probably due to their having been fished in the past by the local inhabitants, coupled with minimal pollution.

Below the Serga inflow, down to Varzuga village, the river presents a typical pastoral view, with its floodplain covered with enclosed fields, haystacks and the occasional log cabin. Most of the riverside trees have been cut down for their timber. This deforestation has resulted in the land immediately adjacent to Varzuga village, with its impressive, wooden, Orthodox 'All Saints church of 1674, having a barren appearance; its soil being highly unstable and blowing up in clouds in the wind. The deterioration in soil surface is further aggravated by the herds of goats cropping its grassy surface, whilst the winter frosts and ice add further to its demise. The resultant sandy dust is carried into the river which becomes discoloured below the village, mussel populations in this area down to the river mouth being infrequent.

Throughout the trip down river Margaritifera were present throughout the length of Varzuga river, but apparently absent from the tributaries. Similarly, salmon parr were also present throughout the length of the Varzuga, yet appear to be scarce in the tributaries. This absence is possibly explained by the turbidity of the water being unsuitable for mussel or salmon parr survival, regardless of apparently suitable substrates being present. Another possible factor for their absence could be winter ice movements in the tributaries.

From my observations it would appear that there is indeed a correlation between mussel and salmon stocks and for this reason it would seem to me to be highly desirable that some form of protection could be afforded to this river system. Such action would ensure that further scientific studies can be carried out, at the same time conserving, with all its associated mussel and salmon stocks, perhaps one of the best natural river systems left in Europe.

AUTHOR'S CONCLUSION

Finally, the author, in response to the recent Recommendation approved by the Ministerial Committee of the Council of Europe in April 1987 on the establishment of computerised data banks, is attempting as a matter of the utmost urgency, to establish an international network aimed to co-ordinate workers and projects engaged on the various aspects of freshwater bivalve research. Emphasis would be given to those concerned with the larger pearly freshwater-mussels, the Naiades, but other freshwater bivalve groups could also be included, e.g. **Corbiculids, Egerids, Sphaerids, Pisids,** etc.

It is intended that UNIO* will promote and co- ordinate research and disseminate information on freshwater-bivalves to both individuals and organisations on a worldwide basis. As a result it is hoped that such action will lead to the establishment of a co-ordinated strategy for the future conservation of this important and severely threatened element of Mollusca.

In order to achieve this it is suggested that the program should include the following:

Firstly, taxonomy, since unless we can readily identify the individual species of animals concerned, we have little chance of being in a position to decide their current status or produce conservation plans. It is imperative, therefore, that relevant experts should be encouraged to produce suitable multilingual identification keys for critical groups and that these should be in a form suitable for general laboratory and field use, by both amateur and professional alike.

Secondly, population and distribution surveys to assess the present and former status of individual species, are also urgently required. It is essential that any vouched specimens resulting from field surveys

*the Universal Naiad Information Organization (UNIO)

are lodged in a museum, or other similar institution, and that this information as to their location is included in the published report on the survey. In this way it is relatively easy for future research workers to verify identifications, or to use any anatomical vouched material thus obtained, which is essential for critical systematic and anatomical studies, at the same time reducing the need to collect further material and thus assisting in the species conservation. It must also be emphasised that reliable surveys can only be achieved once identifications are standardised. In the case of the Scottish BRISC survey, members of the general public were informed of the survey and asked to participate, using the BRISC survey information leaflet and record cards provided, examples of which are given in this book (Appendix 1).

Thirdly, to encourage studies on the biology and habitat requirements, both natural and in captivity, of individual species. This can be accelerated by the production of provisional data sheets on individual species, especially endangered ones, outlining their food and habitat requirements, life histories, and so on. In the majority of cases there will be virtually no information available, thus offering an opportunity for professional and amateur alike to undertake essential original research, which is so essential if we wish to formulate suitable conservation programs, necessary to ensure their future survival.

Fourthly, the Trust hopes to promote an awareness of existing legislation through displays, publicity leaflets and publications, such as the present work. In addition, it is hoped that the Trust will assist in formulating additional proposals for future consideration by the appropriate legislative bodies. These could also include trade and exploitation of molluscs in general, as well as providing an advisory and educational service to statutory bodies, legislative enforcement agencies, etc.

Fifthly, the Trust hopes to stimulate research into commercial freshwater mussel farming, in order to provide nuclei for the cultured pearl industry.

In addition, considerable work needs to be done to determine the use of freshwater bivalves as food; in water purification; as potential environmental monitoring agents, e.g. for copper /magnesium, uranium uptake, or acid rain determination using annual shell layers; in medicine for the determination of Blood groups, coagulating agents, etc; or for their Captive breeding potential, especially in the case of critically endangered species.

In regard to the UNIO Trust establishing an International Network, this already exists in an informal way through the author's involvement in current faunal survey work being undertaken on behalf of the European Invertebrate Survey and also through contacts in Russia, North and South America, Africa, Singapore, Australia and New Zealand.

APPENDIX

BRISC
Biological Recording in Scotland Campaign

FRESHWATER MUSSEL SURVEY

PEARL MUSSEL
Margaritifera margaritifera (L.)

Pollution in Europe has reduced most freshwater mussel populations to critical levels. Recent E.E.C. legislation now provides some protection on the continent for the most endangered species, the Pearl Mussel.

It has been assumed that Scottish freshwater mussels continue to flourish, unaffected by the problems which menace their European relatives. However, there is little evidence for such complacency.

Careful recording of the present distribution of mussels can give early warning of species in danger. We need your help to gather information on freshwater mussels in Scotland, so that we can determine their distribution and status, and thus have the raw materials to ensure their conservation.

Living mussels, despite their size are often inconspicuous, lying half-buried in the gravel or sandy beds of rivers, burns, canals, ponds and lochs.

They live in groups (colonies) and generally remain in the same section of the water body.

WHAT YOU CAN DO

We require **your** records of living mussels or empty shells - but
REMEMBER, ultimately we are interested in live mussels, so even
if you only find empty or fished shells, look for a live colony
nearby.

You are likely to find:
   *A colony of living mussels
   *Empty shells in the shallows or waters edge
   *A number of shells on the bank (evidence of pearl
   fishing)

Once you have located the mussels, follow the survey guidelines
below:

WHAT HAVE YOU FOUND?

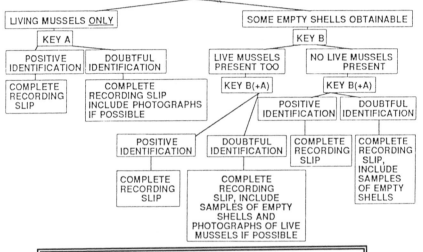

ON NO ACCOUNT COLLECT LIVE MUSSELS!
Only pick up a live mussel if no empty shells are available for
identification. Disturbance of the habitat should be kept to a
minimum. Return mussels to their original position.

IDENTIFICATION OF FRESHWATER MUSSELS

Freshwater mussels present many identification problems. If
positive field identification is not possible, using the keys overleaf,
it is important to send empty shells to the scheme organiser. If
empty shells are unobtainable, a colour photograph of one in the
hand (for scale) will provide additional information when
accompanied by a completed recording slip. Photographs of habitat
and pearl fishing evidence would also be welcomed.

IDENTIFICATION OF FRESHWATER MUSSELS

Features of value in identifying the shells of the Scottish species are:

- Shell colour
- Shell size
- Localised thickening of shell
- Habitat where found
- Hinge teeth (shell interior)

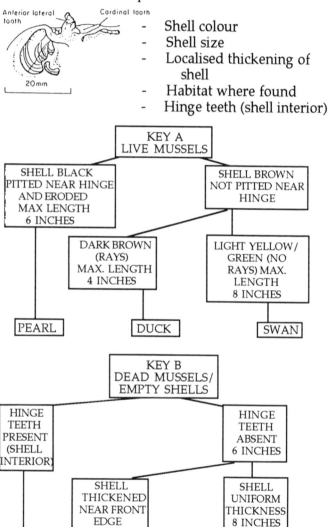

KEY A
LIVE MUSSELS

SHELL BLACK
PITTED NEAR HINGE
AND ERODED
MAX LENGTH
6 INCHES

SHELL BROWN
NOT PITTED NEAR
HINGE

DARK BROWN
(RAYS)
MAX. LENGTH
4 INCHES

LIGHT YELLOW/
GREEN (NO
RAYS) MAX.
LENGTH
8 INCHES

PEARL

DUCK

SWAN

KEY B
DEAD MUSSELS/
EMPTY SHELLS

HINGE
TEETH
PRESENT
(SHELL
INTERIOR)

HINGE
TEETH
ABSENT
6 INCHES

SHELL
THICKENED
NEAR FRONT
EDGE

SHELL
UNIFORM
THICKNESS
8 INCHES

PEARL

DUCK

SWAN

PEARL MUSSEL
Margaritifera margaritifera (L.)
Prefers soft water. Usually found in clean, fast flowing rivers and streams. Shell blackish on outside, often eroded near hinge. Teeth present inside hinge. Length up to 6 inches.

DUCK MUSSEL
Anodonta anatina (L.)
Prefers hard, flowing water, although sometimes found in ponds or lakes. Shell olive brown with darker rays, and thicker near front edge. This can be seen when held up to light. Length up to 4 inches.

SWAN MUSSEL
Anodonta cygnaea (L.)
Prefers hard water. Found on muddy bottoms of slow rivers, canals, lakes and ponds. Shell usually yellowish green without darker rays. Shell of uniform thickness. Length up to 8 inches.

FRESHWATER MUSSEL RECORDING SCHEME
INFORMATION REQUIRED

Survey returns should include a completed recording slip placed inside each bag of shells from the site. If no empty shells are obtainable, simply return the completed slips with photographs if possible.

Shells are delicate and easily damaged, special care must be taken when sending materials by post. If the mussels are dead, scrape out the flesh before posting.

Survey returns should be sent to the scheme organiser at the address below. Postage will be reimbursed if necessary.

> F. R. Woodward
> Glasgow Art Gallery and Museum
> Kelvingrove
> Glasgow
> G3 8AG

CAUTION
EXERCISE GREAT CARE NEAR WATER

BRISC Freshwater Mussel Survey

SUPPORTED BY

WWF

is grant-aided by the World Wide Fund for Nature

Further information on this and other surveys can be obtained from the BRISC office at the address below.

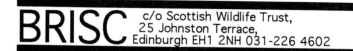

BRISC c/o Scottish Wildlife Trust, 25 Johnston Terrace, Edinburgh EH1 2NH 031-226 4602

FRESHWATER MUSSEL RECORDING SCHEME

INFORMATION REQUIRED

Please fill in the details of the area where the shells are found. Tear off each label and place inside each bag of samples from the site. (If no specimens were obtainable simply return the labels). If a site looks promising but no shells are seen the organiser would still like to know so nil returns are also welcome.

Post shells or information to the scheme organiser:

> F. R. Woodward, Glasgow Museum, Kelvingrove, Glasgow, G3 8AG

Postage will be reimbursed if necessary.

*A
sample form
is shown overleaf
which may be
photocopied
rather than
ripped out
the book*

Name of water body	Nearest town or village	O.S. map ref

Habitat (please tick)

canal	fast flowing	sand	Notes (continue overleaf)
pond	slow moving	mud	
loch	still water	shingle	
river	trees overhanging	boulders	
stream	aquatic plants present near bank		

Pearl fishing?	What evidence?

Fish known?

Trout	Minnow	Stickleback	others

Date	Name of recorder

INDEX